Convergence
Summing All Things Up In Christ

By David Croom

CON**V**ERGENCE
@ JESUS LABS

For More Information About Jesus Labs Visit Us:

www.jesuslabs.org

Prayer and Dedication

All that I have and all that I am is Christ! He has captured my heart and I pray this work will bring us closer to His purpose and will for each of us as Christ is formed in us.

We are the Body of Christ Jesus, The Lord!

I pray for strength, courage and love to abound in Christ to our brothers and sisters across the planet that are suffering for the sake of the gospel. May God bless those who are persecuting you with a revelation of the Lord Jesus Christ.

Thank you for your service and may the God of peace crush Satan under our feet shortly!

For the readers of this book we pray a prayer for the power of the Holy Spirit to light a fire in you to know your purpose in Christ and may the love of our Father flow in and through you in all supernatural knowledge, wisdom and revelation of our glorious inheritance in Christ.

Thank you to the Lamb of God for all You have done for us!

David Croom
A servant of the Lord Jesus Christ

Contents

Introduction
Vision Casting

The rapid multiplication of the first century followers of Jesus Christ was the result of men and women being gripped by a vision. They were living witnesses to the Lordship of Jesus Christ and their lives were the result of celebrating Him. In order to mobilize others, we need to bring them into an encounter with God so they can bear witness of Him with an unshakable conviction. That is the key to making the good news a viral movement.

The purpose of this book is not academic or theoretical. The object is to focus our attention on God's purpose for our lives and learn from Him how He wills to use our time on this planet. The stakes are high, and God is calling ordinary people into an extraordinary plan.

> *"We know that we are of God, and the whole world lies under the sway of the wicked one."* **1 John 5:19**

Numerous movies have been released since the 1950's about alien invasions of the earth. They are really echoing a circumstance that occurred roughly 6000 years ago in a garden in Eden. It was that day a fallen angel infected the thinking and ultimately the DNA of mankind. As a result, all of creation has been subjected to a curse and is waiting for the awakening, rebirth, and revelation of the sons of God. Mankind is born into captivity and does not even realize that there is an ancient war being waged for our inheritance.

If we found that aliens had invaded the Earth and all our friends, neighbors and family were being mind-controlled by some strange device on their heads, we would not be passive or simply attend meetings to theorize about how they will someday, "see the light." Neither would we meet around a piano singing about flying away some day. We would take action.

We have received amazing gifts, power, weapons and even a new identity in Christ that enables us to withstand the cosmic usurpers. We are to use these to assist our fellow inhabitants to discover their destiny in Christ and be free from mind-blindness and oppression. We have also received a mandate to help them integrate into the culture of Heaven and strip off the false identity placed on them in their captivity.

The objective is not to simply free people from the wicked one, but rather bring them into an encounter with the Spirit of Christ and rapidly transform them into fellow laborers. We must rapidly equip and mobilize them to help their friends and family be both free and mobilized to free more people.

You may be surprised to discover that before becoming the adversary of mankind, Lucifer was the top-covering cherub who stood before God night and day. His main function was to steward the glory and revelation of God. He began to trade upon his access and ability to lift or raise his wings and cover the glory. He let iniquity enter his heart.

Lucifer had a close relationship with the pre-incarnate Son and quite possibly his anger towards the bride of Christ is the result of jealousy and bitterness through perceived rejection. God did not reject Lucifer directly. He had no choice but to cast him down when sin was found in him.

He was eventually thrown out of heaven along with one third of the angels that followed him. He then turned his attention on dominating God's companions at the garden in Eden.

It was in this garden that God placed the man Adam and gave him dominion or kingship over the world. It was also here that through a twisting of God's Word, the adversary was able to convince Eve and then Adam to trade with him. In this instance, they made a decision to trade their birthright and inheritance for a meal. This was the only food God had told them was not good. Satan is the name given to this fallen angel. It means "accuser." It was at this point iniquity (doing your own thing) entered into humanity and Satan had indirectly stolen the authority of the kingdom of the world.

A curse was placed upon mankind, upon creation in general, and upon the adversary (Satan). The curse, however, was not permanent. It was conditional upon the coming of Eve's seed:

> "And I will put enmity between you and the woman, And between your seed and her Seed; He shall bruise your head, And you shall bruise His heel." **Genesis 3:15**

This is the victory that was won on the cross. It was the ultimate trade. God became manifest in the flesh, laid His sinless life down for us, and was raised as the first fruit of the new humanity. His victory was so effective that He literally made a public spectacle of principalities and powers.

Many wonder how the devil still has the world under his sway since he is defeated. That is the main point of this book. If we grasp the truth about our mutual authority in Christ and our mandate to further the Kingdom of God, we will hasten the coming restoration of all things and the unburdening of all creation.

> "For the earnest expectation of the creation eagerly waits for the revealing of the sons of God." **Romans 8:19**

The challenge before us is to realize that there is something much bigger at stake than is commonly understood. There are many good intentions and much activity aimed at building Christian organizations and Churches. That is fine and good, but the time is now for the Body of Christ to reach maturity and begin walking as ONE MAN in a unified manifestation of the Son of God as many members.

The Body of Christ must come into the full knowledge of our inheritance in Christ in order to stand against work of the adversary in the immediate future. The challenge is not whether God is able to overcome, but rather; are we aligned, aware and positioned in such a way that God can overcome through us? That is the Lord's viewpoint and His plan: **through us!**

The world is soon to be meeting with tribulation and shaking such as has never been seen before as the end of the ages draws near.

The Holy Spirit is moving us beyond engaging the spiritual realm once or twice a week in church meetings to reveal within us His mandate and instructions to release the Kingdom of God into every area of our lives. The enemy is holding the world captive, and it is our call and destiny to resist the devil. The Third Reich and Hitler were not defeated by large organized armies, but rather by focused members of the underground resistance.

Those believers who are satisfied to sit on their blessed assurance and hope for the rapture are in for quite a shock. Many of our brothers and sisters in Christ live daily in tribulation and persecution for their faith. The martyrs are many, and the reality is that we must all become engaged, equipped, and prepared to be the resistance.

> *"Submit yourselves, then, to God. **Resist the devil**, and he will flee from you."* **James 4:7**

Convergence – Summing Up All Things In Christ

God has incredible exploits planned for each of us who believe. There are tools and resources available to those who will embrace the call to further the Kingdom of God and to stand against the wiles of the devil. This requires a commitment far greater than simply agreeing to attend a church program, pass out fliers, or sing songs. We must embrace the cross of our Lord Jesus and get over ourselves.

The power of the message of the cross enables us to, "not love our lives to the death." This is the power of an over-comer. This same power enables us to lay our lives down for one another.

> "And war broke out in heaven: Michael and his angels fought with the dragon; and the dragon and his angels fought, but they did not prevail, nor was a place found for them in heaven any longer. So the great dragon was cast out, that serpent of old, called the Devil and Satan, who deceives the whole world; he was cast to the earth, and his angels were cast out with him.
>
> Then I heard a loud voice saying in heaven, "Now salvation, and strength, and the kingdom of our God, and the power of His Christ have come, for the accuser of our brethren, who accused them before our God day and night, has been cast down. **And they overcame him by the blood of the Lamb and by the word of their testimony, and they did not love their lives to the death.** Therefore rejoice, O heavens, and you who dwell in them! Woe to the inhabitants of the earth and the sea! For the devil has come down to you, having great wrath, because he knows that he has a short time." **Revelation 12:7-11**

Over time, men have changed the name and nature of what we call the Church and have diluted the power of the Body of Christ. The Kingdom of God is represented in the Body of Christ and not through a religious or political organization.

We are to be both equipped and empowered to demonstrate God's manifold wisdom to principalities and powers in this world and to release the Government of God into the heavenly realms.[1] The world is in moral decay and disaster. Our destiny empowers us to bring the anointing of God as Christ is embodied in our lives.

It is estimated that 70,000 people die every day. This is truly a spiritual holocaust as more than 20 million people a year are dying. The tragedy is that they are dying still captive to Satan and entering eternity condemned along with him.

As the end of the ages draws near, we are blessed to co-labor with the Holy Spirit as He engages in the business of declaring the Kingdom and Government of God in all areas of our lives and spheres of influence. The god of this age is still blinding minds to the light and glory of the good news. We must have compassion on the captives around us and engage the enemy outside the limits of "church services" and programs.

God's Creative Power

The conflict between Chaos and Logos

> "In the beginning God created the heavens and the earth. Now the earth was formless and empty, darkness was over the surface of the deep, and the Spirit of God was hovering over the waters." **Genesis 1:1-2**

There is no power or authority greater than God. The worldly idea that the opposite of God is Satan, sin or evil is incorrect. God's nature at the core is order. Their act of creation has brought order to chaos. The Spirit moves from "hovering over the waters" of the deep or "chaos" to creating order out of chaos by the power of the Word.

Satan is still roaming around and both sin and death still exist because God is still creating. When we understand that creation is the power of the Word of God to create order from chaos, it becomes clear that there is still chaos needing to be brought into subjection to the will of God.

Adam's original mandate was to continue the work of creating order from chaos. He was co-creating the nature of animals through the delegated authority of naming.

Once the fall occurred, the mandate remained but was made more difficult by the new limitations and curses upon the earth. This was when the Cosmos or world system was created. This is the overlying system that Satan still controls. The mandate has been passed to each member of the Body of Christ. All authority in Heaven and Earth belongs to Jesus Christ and He is with us always to the end of the age.

The Holy Spirit will empower us to embody the continuing ministry of Jesus Christ in serving the inhabitants of this planet and to bring forth His inheritance in the saints.
The mission is great and our hope is in the power of God.

> *"Do we begin again to commend ourselves? Or do we need, as some others, epistles of commendation to you or letters of commendation from you? You are our epistle written in our hearts, known and read by all men; clearly you are an epistle of Christ, ministered by us, written not with ink but by the Spirit of the living God, not on tablets of stone but on tablets of flesh, that is, of the heart. The Spirit, Not the Letter.*
>
> *And we have such trust through Christ toward God. Not that we are sufficient of ourselves to think of anything as being from ourselves, but our sufficiency is from God, who also made us sufficient as ministers of the new covenant, not of the letter but of the Spirit; for the letter kills, but the Spirit gives life."* **2 Corinthians 3:1-6**

Catalyzing A Movement

The primary action we can take is to ask the Lord what His plan is for our friends, families, neighbors, city, nation and planet. As He speaks to us we simply respond to His instructions.

Persecution was commonly the catalyst to the multiplication of believers in the early church and is seen in the rapid multiplying of believers in places like China today. Aggressive persecution and serious consequences for discovery set an environment for a thriving, focused and engaging culture of believers.

Being a catalyst means we are bringing the spark of the fire of God to others. We need not wait for persecution to become a relevant subversive force in our current culture.

Our intention is not to take ownership of God's movement in people's lives, but rather to light a fire. The fire is in the field of the harvest and cannot be controlled. The wind of the Holy Spirit will cause the fire to multiply and burn away the old creation in Adam and bring forth the new creation in Christ.

There are many methods and books about starting new worship services. This book is concerned with engaging the population with the good news of Jesus Christ without any religious, social or organizational limits. Movement is organic decentralized, subversive, relational, mobile and alive.

We are putting into action ancient principles and strategies revealed in the patterns of Jesus and the first century believers as they produced transformational disciple-making communities.

Convergence – Summing Up All Things In Christ

Jesus Christ is Lord and all authority under heaven and Earth belongs to Him. The good news is that we are called to participate in this with Him. The doorway into this participation is to bow our knee and declare that He is Lord. It is then that we are saved. While the world remains under the sway of the wicked one, those who belong to the Son are free indeed.[2]

God has chosen ordinary people that the world sees as "not qualified" or foolish to accomplish His amazing purpose. This book is for people who know there is more to the abundant life of Christ than endless meetings and talking.

The Holy Spirit is inspiring and enabling us to walk in an apostolic vision that views the world around us through the lens of mission and purpose. This requires us to shift into a different way of living and thinking that is fueled and energized by the Spirit and His plan for us as the Body of Christ.

Satan has no power over the over-comers. We are the joy-filled, no-death-fearing, neighbor loving, friends-of-sinners, Spirit filled brothers and sisters of the Lord Jesus Christ!

We invite you to join us on a subversive journey of adventure, suffering and glory. It is through the power of God's Spirit that we endure all things for the sake of the gospel.

Jesus Christ is the creator of the universe that spans trillions of galaxies. He can take us on an adventure further than we can think or imagine. We have an unexplainable joy and abundance of hope as God reveals His master plan to bring all things into alignment and point the attention of the universe to see Christ manifested through the sons of God.

Chapter One

THE CONVERGENCE

(kun-vûrjens) Noun: The degree or point at which lines, objects, etc., converge.

The term CONVERGENCE identifies the exact nature of God's work in the world today. He is converging all the forces of the universe upon specific individuals with an intended purpose of conforming us to the image of Christ. The Father is gathering to Himself people called according to His eternal purpose.

> *"And we know that all things work together for good to those who love God, to those who are the called according to His purpose. For whom He foreknew, He also predestined to be conformed to the image of His Son, that He might be the firstborn among many brethren. Moreover whom He predestined, these He also called; whom He called, these He also justified; and whom He justified, these He also glorified."* **Romans 8:28-30**

Destined For Glory

Our destiny in Christ is reaching out of eternity and bringing us into the power of the stream of God's will. There is a key principle to living a victorious Christian life that has been hidden in plain sight. It is a mystery that God has now revealed to us by removing the veil and the strongholds blocking our view from His enormous goodness and grace.

It is our faith and desire that through the ancient and eternal principles revealed in the following pages, God will shift your thinking and bring you into alignment with the tremendous force of God's blessing, power and provision.

Convergence is defined as the point of intersection that sums up all lines or streams into a single point. This could also describe the Headship of Jesus Christ. God is summing up all things in Christ. He has re-created us in Christ as a community of believers moving in the dynamic of His purpose and drawing life from His Headship.

Christ Is Head of the Body

The Lord's function as Head of the Body is not about government, but rather about life. He is the center and source for everything. In Him all things consist.

To properly understand the principle of Christ being the Head of the Body, we must look at the origin of the word for head. The Greek word for "head" is κεφαλή - kephale.[3] Kephale appears to have been primarily used in two contexts. First it is the actual head of a living organism and second it would apply as the source of something.[4] The source of a river for example, would be a kephale. This is a very good way to describe the function of the Headship of Christ.

Christ is our life and our source. When we know Christ as our source, it makes no sense for us to place a human being in between His Body, the Head Himself and us. Paul says we are to grab hold of the Head to be fed or nourished. The Lord called Himself the Way, the Truth and the Life. The path and the goal are both tied up in a Person.

The very moment we have a believing encounter with and confess Jesus as Lord, we are leaving behind our self-focused life for an interdependent life as a member of the Body of Christ. Our identity is Christ. It is no longer our life to live, but His to express in and through us.

As we draw on Christ as our source, we exchange our individual life for one of interdependence in His Body. The basis of the exchange is covenant. The New Covenant is an agreement between two parties to pool their resources. He takes all that we have and gives us all that belongs to Himself. This is an exchange occurring outside the parameters of time and space. He takes our sin and self and brings them into death through the cross. When He rises again we are all included in the benefits and power of His Sonship by our being placed in Christ.

The principle of convergence is God's power working through each member of His Body by the power of the Spirit of Life to process us into a full and expressed union with Christ until His image is clearly being broadcast among us.

Community Incubator

God uses community as an incubator to form Christ in us. Just as a new baby is immersed in the "human" culture, we need to be immersed in Heaven's culture. The separation of personal and spiritual lives has starved the Body of Christ and left orphaned babies all over the place. The Holy Spirit is working all things together for His purpose and there is tremendous benefit in joining Him.

Much suffering and discipline could be avoided if we were simply tuned into the frequency that God is broadcasting and live our lives in harmony with God's plan. He has chosen us in Christ with a plan and a purpose. When we realize the goal is to mature us and conform us to the image of Christ then we can focus on His work to do just that. He does the work and we follow His lead. It is that simple.

When we are moving in the light and power of His Headship, we are a Christ-Centered community. The relational dimension of this community is so dynamic that it can feel like walking in a constant state of déjà vu. Déjà Vu is French word describing a feeling that we have already experienced an event as it is transpiring. The collective mindset of a community plugged into the Holy Spirit will be marked by constant and amazing coincidences.

 A coincidence occurs as two events are occurring at one time. This is possible because God has already prepared the works and pathways beforehand that WE should walk in them.

> "Your eyes saw my substance, being yet unformed. And in Your book they all were written, the days fashioned for me, when as yet there were none of them." **Psalm 139:16**

Convergence occurs as we walk out God's eternal purpose and ordinary events become extraordinary supernatural encounters. Our daily rhythms of life become one supernatural event after another. All the forces of the universe are converging together to move us towards God eternal purpose: A many-member image. Just as a TV screen is made up of thousands of pixels or crystals. Not one of us more important than the other, but each of us are equally necessary to complete the picture as God is broadcasting Christ through us to the universe.

> *"In Him we have redemption through His blood, the forgiveness of sins, according to the riches of His grace which He made to abound toward us in all wisdom and prudence, having made known to us the mystery of His will, according to His good pleasure which He purposed in Himself, that in the dispensation of the fullness of the times He might gather together in one all things in Christ, both which are in heaven and which are on earth in Him."* **Ephesians 1:7-10**

> *"And we know that all things work together for good to those who love God, to those who are the called according to His purpose. For whom He foreknew, He also predestined to be conformed to the image of His Son, that He might be the firstborn among many brethren. Moreover whom He predestined, these He also called; whom He called, these He also justified; and whom He justified, these He also glorified."* **Romans 8:28-30**

As we fully grasp the direction of God's will, we can see that His will is not tied up in making us happy or fixing up the things that are wrong in our life. He is working something eternal in us that transcends this life. He is exchanging our old life for one in the new creation. Paul said that our light affliction works for us a far greater weight of glory.[5]

God's eternal purpose is not about you or me. The "I" is crucified in Christ and there is a new being that is no longer an individual, but rather a member of Christ. Christ in us is now our life and God is working all things together to bring us all into the fullness of the measure of Christ.

Ekklesia – The Called

Nowhere in the New Testament do we find the word church referring to a building or a place you go. It may come as a surprise to know that the word "church" never actually occurs in the original language of the Bible. The Greek word used is ekklēsia (Ekklesia).[6] The use of the word church has become so watered down over time that it has become known as a religious organization or building. When we talk about church it is crucial that we realize that the church is not a place or something we do, it is our identity. We followers of Jesus Christ are the Church, the Body of Christ.

> **According to the Encyclopedia Britannica:**
> "In the New Testament, "ekklesia" (signifying convocation) is the only single word used for church. It (ekklesia) was the name given to the governmental assembly of the city of Athens, duly convoked (called out) by proper officers and possessing all political power including even judicial functions."
>
> *"And He put all things under His feet, and gave Him to be head over all things to the church, which is His body, the fullness of Him who fills all in all."* **Ephesians 1:22-23**

When the Lord Jesus told Peter that He would build His (Church) Ekklesia on the rock of revelation,[7] He was not talking about a religious organization. His context was the existing Roman government as expressed through an ekklesia. When Rome conquered a country or region in battle they would assign the ekklesia into that region. The ekklesia was actually a called out governing body. This was a twofold assignment. They were to represent the Roman government's authority as well as teaching the newly acquired citizens to think and act like Romans. The Ekklesia of God has the same assignment in respect to ruling over the heavenly places and representing the culture of the Kingdom of God in the world.

When the Lord said He would build His Ekklesia, He used the Greek word: οἰκοδομέω (oikodomeō). The word is two parts and means to "house build."[8] God is in effect building a Royal Family of Kings and Priests.

To fully understand the context of a Roman ekklesia we could compare it to a modern senatorial government. In the Book of Acts we see the Kingdom of God multiplying rapidly and the Senate of God growing in authority. This is why there was so much animosity towards the believers. In **Acts 17:6** they were, "Turning the world upside down." Just as we confer a great degree of status and respect upon Senators in the United States Government, how much more value should be placed upon the members of the Senate of the Kingdom of God?

The Ekklesia is a living organism. We are each connected to one another as we are connected to Jesus Christ, the Head of the Body. A key paradigm shift in the New Covenant is that we are called out of our individual lives and into the community of the Body of Christ. **Colossians 3:4** "Christ Who is our Life." Christ is our life -- not my or your life, but ours. We share in His life.

The first century Ekklesia shared all things in common. While that may not be the result of our community, just as they experienced Him together, we can and should expect to live with "one mind," "one heart," and "one soul." We all share the same life and that life is Christ: He is our life.

The Ekklesia is not an institution or an organization. It is a household. We are all born into the family business. It is a royal household and our business is to serve the inhabitants of this planet as we serve Christ.

Christ In Us Is The Hope of Glory

The Church/Ekklesia is the Body of Christ. Where the Church is, there is Christ and where Christ is, there is the Church, His Body. We are forever connected, as two who are married become one flesh, or rather, one Body.

> " For we are members of His body, of His flesh and of His bones. "For this reason a man shall leave his father and mother and be joined to his wife, and the two shall become one flesh. "This is a great mystery, but I speak concerning Christ and the church." **Ephesians 5:30-32**

The Ekklesia is universal in that we are members of the Body of Christ. The only division of churches/ekklesias found in the New Testament was by region or city. There is one Ekklesia per city. For example, "The church that is in Cornith" or "the church of the Laodiceans."

There are many ways of gathering and expressing the Ekklesia. There are many local gatherings, but in the Spirit, there is no division. When we take ownership of the Ekklesia by calling it "my" or "our" church, we reveal that we do not understand that we are all God's household and any division is caused by our own "us" and "them" creation.

People choose where to "go to church" for many personal preferences and reasons. The Holy Spirit will guide us into relationships that transcend our personal preferences. It would do us well in removing the phrase, "go to church" from our vocabulary because it perpetuates the idea of a location being the goal and not our identity.

There is a sense of communitas that develops among people who go through a challenge together. This is a deep comradre seen in the military. We should seek the same communitas with other households or relational communities as we take responsibility together for the spiritual condition of our cities.

What distinctly defines a city is proximity. This includes people and their living spaces, workplaces, and cultural institutions. It also encompasses street life and marketplaces. This is what the first century believers knew to be a "city."

When the Lord Jesus spoke to the ekklesia's in **Revelation 3**, He referred to them by region and city and held them collectively accountable for their spiritual condition. It also appears there is an angelic overseer of each regional ekklesia.

> "'And to the angel of the church of the Laodiceans write, 'These things says the Amen, the Faithful and True Witness, the Beginning of the creation of God: 'I know your works, that you are neither cold nor hot. I could wish you were cold or hot. So then, because you are lukewarm, and neither cold nor hot I will vomit you out of My mouth. Because you say, 'I am rich, have become wealthy, and have need of nothing'—and do not know that you are wretched, miserable, poor, blind, and naked— I counsel you to buy from Me gold refined in the fire, that you may be rich; and white garments, that you may be clothed, that the shame of your nakedness may not be revealed; and anoint your eyes with eye salve, that you may see. As many as I love, I rebuke and chasten. Therefore be zealous and repent. Behold, I stand at the door and knock. If anyone hears My voice and opens the door, I will come in to him and dine with him, and he with Me. To him who overcomes I will grant to sit with Me on My throne, as I also overcame and sat down with My Father on His throne. 'He who has an ear, let him hear what the Spirit says to the churches.'" **Ephesians 3:14-22**

We are all connected as members of His Body and when one of us is misaligned, the whole Body locally and globally is affected.

The 99% Principle

We are living in a time of radical growth in technology and science. This new millennium is marked by a meteoric rise in communication and information through cellular and Internet technologies.[9] We have more than enough information and the world is being overtaken by its desire for comfort and the ease of instant entertainment. The problem is that this flow of information and entertainment is connected to a frequency that has its root in the god of this age. The book of James calls this the wisdom from below. John tells us that the world is under the sway of the wicked one.

Consequently, God is calling out His people and releasing us into His purpose. God's eternal purpose started before the fall of Adam. Our message is therefore, one of great news. The gospel is a God-focused message of His desire for reconciliation and God is reconciling the world to Himself through us. We have the power to engage the world with truth encounters that are based on the reality of God's presence. He is the Truth and makes Himself known through us.

This is an era of new age spirituality and there is an increasingly popular desire for spiritual experiences. The spiritual experiences, however, are mostly self-focused and the experience is the end goal. They are the fruit of individualism born in the garden in Eden. They are focused on individualism and self-empowerment. Much of the spirituality, even in what are called churches, is not associated with responsibility or caring for others.

The experiences result in meetings that seem more like a performance with a few professionals functioning and passive seated spectators. The result is not empowering people to go make disciples, but rather to have more meetings.

It is quite possible the Holy Spirit has directed you to this material because you have been a passive spectator or even one of the few functioning professionals. The point is that neither side of this coin is empowering the Body of Christ to engage the culture.

Spirit filled meetings and gatherings are good for us. The issue is that the 1-2 hours a week spent in these "church meetings" adds up to about 1% of the 168 hours in a week. That leaves us 99% of our time to engage the world as ambassadors of Heaven. The Lord is working in our lives to engage the world for Christ with tremendous power and effectiveness. It is our part to join Him in His mission.

Putting Our Faith Into Action

The Holy Spirit will reveal to us both the work of the cross of our Lord Jesus Christ and the way of the cross in laying our lives down for one another. If our spiritual Christian experience goes no further than getting goose bumps, we may need to invest in a sweater. An encounter with the Holy Spirit will always fill us with His compassion for others. Compassion is God's love moving us to action.

Our most spiritual meetings will not impact the world. Meetings, programs, and events do not make disciples. Disciples who are bearing fruit make disciples. If we never get outside of meetings, we can never truly bear fruit by making disciples who make disciples.

We have already seen that meetings and services comprise 1% of our available week. While there is a need for personal ministry, we have found that centering on a single person's gift limits the prophetic power of our gathering together.
If a group of 100 people center on a single "teacher," the

atmosphere is at 1% effectiveness or 1 out of a 100.
Imagine what it would be like if everyone were to participate
and the gifts of the spirit were operating at full capacity. That is
the model that Paul introduced in 1 Corinthians 14. There is a
context for teaching meetings, but that cannot be our only
context. Spectators are not really participants, so if this is our
only context, we are limiting the prophetic potential of our
gathering.

So far we are seeing how some are operating at 1%
effectiveness with 1% of their time. Knowing that it is God's will
to engage the world through us, we can be much more
effective by shifting into the stream of God's will in the
convergence. This is not done through programs or systems.
This requires us to be tuned into the Holy Spirit and to co-labor
with Him as He directs us. It His life working purpose into our
relationships and the Holy Spirit manifesting Christ in us.

The other side of the 99% principle is our harmony with the
truth. Much spiritual activity in the West is based on studying
the Scriptures and memorizing them in classroom settings.

How much impact do we have in the world when we can quote
every Scripture in the Bible, but it does impact our relationships
with one another and move us into compassionate action? We
are always in "church" because we are the church. This will be
more evident when we stop using the phrase "go to church."

When we move beyond head knowledge to heart knowledge, it
moves us to apply what we know in serving Christ through
others. The truth should impact us more than curiosity or as
fodder for discussion and move us to lay down our lives for one
another. The gospel will impact every area of our life when we
embrace the truth beyond the meeting place and invite the
world to view Christ in us through the platform of "all things."

Mobilizing Now

God is gathering us together as apostolic "sent ones" who operate from a vision that translates what God is doing into our daily lives. Each one of us can, through the Holy Spirit, see and participate in His work. The Lord will show us the where and the how and our part is to respond in faith to what He shows us.

The example of Jesus was to look and see what the Father was doing. He did not initiate things on His own, but trusted in and experienced His Father's guidance:

> *"Then Jesus answered and said to them, 'Most assuredly, I say to you, the Son can do nothing of Himself, but what He sees the Father do; for whatever He does, the Son also does in like manner. For the Father loves the Son, and shows Him all things that He Himself does; and He will show Him greater works than these, that you may marvel.'"* **John 5:19-20**

We do not need to feel as though we are not doing enough, praying enough, or not meeting self-imposed standards. There is no condemnation for those who are in Christ Jesus. He has plans for us that were prepared before we were even born.

When we turn our minds to the Spirit, He will guide and direct our steps. His work is always relational and He is orchestrating our lives together with a spiritual harmony that produces through us His masterpiece that is the Body of Christ.

GPS - Glory Positioning System

The Lord orders the steps of a righteous man.[10] This is God's GPS. You could also call it His Glory Positioning System. He is positioning us into situations and relationships at specific times and places in order to achieve maximum glory.

We are, by the nature of our call and birthright, both missional and engaged in the world as partners with God in His redemptive mission. The platform is not a building or a neutral location, but rather all areas of our life. If we limit ourselves to a certain schedule or location, we are limited to both time and space. We cannot expect to engage the enemy by conducting endless meetings and talking. The world is under his sway.

Ephesians 2 tells us that we were created in Christ Jesus for good works that He prepared beforehand that WE should walk in them. **The good works are walked out, not worked out.**

Understanding that our lives are not a series of accidental occurrences, but are rather filled with purpose will give us rest. That is important because we are not only seated together in heavenly places, but we are also walking out the good works together. The seating is part of our kingly assignment as kings sit on thrones when they exercise authority. The walking out portion is our on-the-planet priestly assignment in action.

God wrote out our daily planner before the foundation of the world. When we present ourselves to Him and He guides our schedule, we can accomplish so much in our day that people will be amazed. Time and space are for mere mortals. We are the sons of God and function in the river of God's will as each of our life streams converge in Christ.

God's Dwelling

God's eternal purpose is to establish a dwelling place and He is doing this by building us up together. We are the mobile and living stones of this dwelling. Living in the convergence and stream of God's will makes it possible to maintain mobility and multiplication. We are the mobile embassies of God. It is through us that God is reconciling the world. When we are tuned in and responding to the Holy Spirit together, there is tremendous synergy and spiritual power at our disposal.

As Jesus told Nicodemus, we are born of the Spirit and are children of the wind.[11] Just as the wind is invisible, so is the Holy Spirit. We are the leaves and branches moving as He blows that make Him visible to the world around us. God's will is for our lives, our homes and our relationships to be immersed in His presence. Our households are to be His habitation. He does not want to simply visit us at a neutral meeting somewhere, but rather to be central and visible in our day-to-day lives.

Ministry is not something that we must do or add to our schedule. It is the result of seeing our lives on this planet as an extended mission trip. We can then live a life of gospel intentionality in which every event is an opportunity to serve as an ambassador of Heaven.

"As you go, make disciples." **Matthew 28:1**

When we become rooted to a specific location, we begin to box ourselves into a time and space limitation. When we present our schedule to God, He can use us any time and any place to accomplish His will and to manifest His Kingdom.

Rather than simply running errands and shopping, we engage the world as we go. We leave the house to "go and make disciples." As we are out, we accomplish our tasks and pick up what we need. Normal activities then become platforms of supernatural meetings and strategic relationship building occurs everywhere we go. This forward momentum keeps us in the offensive against the world and the forces of darkness. Offensive movement is always our best defensive posture in spiritual warfare.

Once our schedule belongs to God, our time is allotted for His use and not for our flesh. This reality was clearly demonstrated by King David. He won every battle but the one he stayed home from. It was when the armies were out fighting and he remained behind that he experienced his biggest defeat in falling into temptation over Bathsheba.[12]

Community Power

We are children of the light and light dispels darkness by simply overriding it. Our fellowship with one another affords us tremendous advantage. We can walk with such spiritual authority that the enemy dreads to see us coming. When we enter a room, demons should have the same sinking feeling we would get if we see red lights in the rear view mirror of our car and knew we were speeding. They should be hoping we do not turn our attention their way.

What most believers call warfare is really them taking a victim stance. The warfare God has given us is offensive. The gates of hell statement made by the Lord Jesus to Peter meant that His Ekklesia would be taking down the enemy's gates.

> *"And I also say to you that you are Peter, and on this rock I will build My church, and the gates of Hades shall not prevail against it."* **Matthew 16:18**

We should not be maintaining a defensive posture at the local "church building" and hoping the adversary does not see us. We have been given a place of authority and power over such things. We are on a list in the Lamb's book that designates us to have authority over serpents and demons. They fear Christ in us, and through Him we overcome the adversary every time.

The Lordship of Jesus Christ is over all things. He wants more than our Sundays and Wednesday nights. It is His intention to fill every area of our life with His anointing and power. This includes our homes, our offices, and our social platforms. Our life is not our own. The community-shared life of Christ is our inheritance and these areas should be filled with Christ through His Body. Our fellowship with one another empowers us to engage the culture as an embodiment of Christ.

The Convergence

As we all receive Christ inwardly, He becomes our life together. We no longer have a right to our own private life of secrets and selfish desires. He takes up residence inside of believers and has every right to our lives.

The common misconception in the West is that there is a spiritual and a secular life. This is called compartmentalizing. This results in believers living private lives away from other believers and causes a great deal of heartache and defeat.

This is one of many obvious strongholds placed in the culture by the devil. These strongholds include terms like tolerance, political correctness, and relative truth. If he can get people under the umbrella of these concepts, they are already on the bench and not even in the game.

Compartmentalizing is the result of the extraction evangelism model. It is common for new believers to be sought out as individuals and encouraged to "go to church." This limits the growth of new believers as well as the local Body of Christ by extracting the new believer away to a neutral location. It also misses the obvious opportunity to bring the Kingdom of God and the good news into their existing social networks.

We are going to explore the very powerful Oikos principle that was used by the Lord Jesus, His disciples, Paul, and the first century believers. The Holy Spirit would bring them to connectors or "persons of peace" that were in effect bridges to vast networks of new believers. The Household (Oikos) principle is the key to our understanding the relationships of the family and the Kingdom of God.

Not Your Own Life

Community is an essential dynamic of the Christian life. Our communities are the most visible expression of the gospel. As culture reflects the values of its citizens, community reflects the values of the Kingdom of God.

In **John 17:23**, The Lord Jesus clearly stated that it was our love for one another and oneness that would create the atmosphere of faith to make Him visible and tangible to the world.

There is a natural tendency for us to individualize and personalize the letters of the New Testament. The truth is they were almost always addressed and read to a group of listeners. There are thousands of books and videos produced every year teaching, "How I can be a good Christian" and be "Christ-like." These further the misconception of an individual walk with God.

The English translation of the word "you" does not clearly differentiate between singular and plural. The closest plural variant is the word from the American south, "y'all." Paul's letters often used the Greek plural form of you (**humeis**) as they were written and addressed to groups of believers in various regions and cities. For instance, the "you" in "Christ in you, the hope of glory" in **Colossians 1:27**, has in a view the Body of Christ and is not speaking to individuals.[13]

This can also apply to the singular word your as in **Philippians 2:12,** "work out your own salvation with fear and trembling." The context was to work out their salvation among themselves. This salvation is a present reality of our being made whole in body, soul, and spirit. This comes from the word σῴζω (sozo).[14] This wholeness is a community process. We cannot be made whole apart from the other members of the Body of Christ. The work is a community effort through the one another dynamic. Wholeness only comes when we stop trying to "go it alone."

The Bible Was Not Written For Professionals

Keep in mind the Scriptures were not written to professional ministers and leaders to study and filter to the brothers and sisters in Christ. They were read out loud to everyone and were received with mutual edification. Do you need to go to a special school for years to be qualified to read a letter from a friend? The New Testament is made up mostly of letters written to groups of regular people living out the Christ life together who were called into an extraordinary life of power and anointing. They were not theological books, but real letters to people being discipled as on the job apprentices in the school of Christ.

It is the ministry of the Holy Spirit to bring the words to life and to impart life among us. **How often do we gather to simply read the Scriptures in their context and allow the Holy Spirit to bring them to life?** This requires no special skills or training and is one of the primary value containers of a catalyzing a Christ Centered Movement. It is a relational and easy way to duplicate and multiply our communities.

Read the last paragraph again and ask yourself if you are qualified to do this.

The power of reading the Scriptures together is that it eliminates our tendency to individualize them. When we begin to see the Body dynamic in Scriptures that had been previously individualized, it brings us into harmony with the experience of wholeness as members of Christ's Body. Remember, the New Testament letters were written to Christ's Body, not to experts or individuals.

Harvest and Power

Pentecost is commonly associated with the time the Spirit was poured out in the Acts 2 account. The Greek word pentēkostē (penekoste) means "the fiftieth."[15] Fifty concerns the number of days since Passover. It is also called Feast of Weeks, because it falls seven weeks after the First Fruits in which they celebrated the end of the barley harvest and the beginning of the wheat harvest.

The Day of Pentecost has become to us a celebration of the ongoing spiritual harvest.

> *"The harvest is plentiful, but the workers are few. Ask the Lord of the harvest, therefore, to send out workers in His harvest field." Luke 10:2*

The Day of Pentecost started with 120 laborers being empowered with the Holy Spirit and then 3000 more laborers were added through the amazing testimony through Peter of Jesus Christ. The baptism of the Holy Spirit empowers us to declare the good news and to be witnesses of the Lord Jesus Christ.

In the West we commonly see the practice of "soul winning" and the harvest is viewed as getting people saved. The principle of the 99% shows us there is more than enough "ministry" for everyone. The harvest consists of billions of people all around us.

The Lord does not need us to pray for the lost, but rather instructed us to see the harvest as ripe and to pray for the Lord of the Harvest to raise up laborers. It is therefore, not our prayers for the lost, but rather our obedience in praying for laborers that will impact the lost.

*"But you shall receive power when the Holy Spirit has come upon you and you shall be witnesses (martyrs) to Me in Jerusalem and in all Judea and Samaria and to the ends of the earth." **Acts 1:8***

The Father has poured out His Spirit to enable the Body of Christ to reap a spiritual harvest. There is no need to self-initiate the harvest. It was for this reason the Holy Spirit was sent on His current mission on the planet.

The Holy Spirit was sent with a specific intention and mission to prepare us to reap the harvest. When we yield the totality of our lives to His mission, He will use every area of our lives for the gospel. This is living a life with gospel intentionality. The intentionality is in seeking His will and responding as He leads us into our inheritance each day.

The Lord Jesus rose from the dead on the very day of the First Fruits. Celebrating First Fruits is really a celebration of the resurrection of Jesus Christ from the dead. The glorious truth is that we are celebrating Pentecost every day as new believers are added to the Body of Christ and subsequently baptized in the Holy Spirit. James Rutz, the author of Megashift estimates that 3000 new believers are born in the Body of Christ every 25 minutes.[16]

How thrilling is it to know that there is a new Pentecost in the Body of Christ every 25 minutes. That means that it might be quiet in our respective location in time and space, but globally and universally, there is tremendous activity in the Body of Christ. There is no down time in God's Kingdom.

Pentecost is no longer just a twenty-four hour period of time. It is now meant to describe a whole age in which the Body of Christ is at work gathering Christ's inheritance in the saints.

> *"I planted, Apollos watered, but God gave the
> increase. So then neither he who plants is
> anything, nor he who waters, but God who gives
> the increase. Now he who plants and he who
> waters are one, and each one will receive his own
> reward according to his own labor. For we are
> Gods fellow workers; you are Gods field, you are
> Gods building."* **1 Corinthians 3:6-9**

The harvest is riper today than any time in history. We are the laborers called to work in God's field. We can celebrate the Day of Pentecost daily as the Lord of the Harvest raises up more laborers from within the harvest.

Do people define our communities as people who celebrate? Our daily lives should be a demonstration of someone who has heard and is living in the light of very good news.

The Good News and Gospel are the same thing. We are living a life of good news intentionality. If we are really thrilled with the good news of Jesus Christ, it will be obvious everywhere and to everyone.

Harvest Strategies

There were no churches in the New Testament. Did you catch that? There was not one church as we know them today.

What we see in the accounts of first century are Christ-centered communities that meet in various locations and often in houses. There is never a single instance that believers got together and started having formal church services or had fundraisers in order to construct cathedrals or church buildings.

This may account for the viral-like movement of Christ throughout the regions. Today, much of what is considered church planting is the starting of new one or two-hour services to attract and shuffle existing believers from one place or another. There is nothing wrong with such activities if God is directing them. Unless believers are equipped and mobilized beyond meetings, however we are not engaging the world for Christ.

If we gather in remote or neutral locations together, the enemy is certainly not obligated to stop by so we can cast him out. Our objective is to move with the Holy Spirit on His mission to reconcile the world and free others from the devil's power. We are going to look at what happens when we turn our lives into disciple making platforms.

Living a gospel intentional life is a game changer!

The first century pattern taught by the Lord Jesus and exampled in the Book of Acts was household Oikos Evangelism. The Greek word used for this network is OIKOS.[17] It is translated in the gospels as household. In the West this could also be called a social network. This is more than just family members and can include coworkers, clubs, friends,

Facebook or twitter friends, and many other social connections. It is the vehicle or framework that enables the advancing and operation of the (Called Out Governing Body) Ekklesia of Christ.

Luke recorded numerous key people or bridges prepared by the Holy Spirit to believe and their households becoming network hubs to expand the Body of Christ. Keep in the mind the term household is referring to people, not buildings. The power of the Christ Centered lifestyle comes from the Holy Spirit connecting us together with others according to an ancient plan. We are being fitted together as living stones.

Remember, we are not working out the good works prepared for us, but are rather walking them out together.

Other than a couple isolated examples in Acts such as Philip and the Eunuch, the early believers never actually separated evangelism and community. They weren't seen seeking out individuals for the purpose of getting them saved. Neither did they extract people from their network of family and friends, but rather brought the power of the good news to them and their entire extended household. God still uses the pattern of revealing the person of peace or bridges to us in order to bring the gospel <u>through</u> them to their existing networks of relationships.

Letterbox Theology

When we watch movies that were made for the big screen on a smaller television, they must be modified. If there is no letterbox format, the sides are cut off and we miss part of the scenery and some of the characters.

Many Scriptures have been pulled, isolated and stripped of context to fit someone's natural thinking of spiritual matters. As we seek the mind of Christ together, He will expand our understanding and the same Scriptures we have heard for years will suddenly burst alive with potential and power.

Much western Christian teaching perpetuates viewing Scripture through the identity of individualism. As a result, many of us have missed seeing this relational pattern of the Holy Spirit. In the historical record in Scripture, He is seen directing outreach through existing relational networks of the households or Oikos. This is principle is woven deeply into the fabric of the Gospels, Acts and the Epistles. We intend to explore this principle with practical examples and value driven strategies.

The ministry of Jesus clearly demonstrates that He utilized existing relationships to serve as bridges to spread His message and to facilitate access to a network of relationships. In addition, He mobilized the 12 disciples and then the 70 using existing relational networks as the prevailing apostolic protocol.

The power of God's converging power to sum up all things in Christ is directed through these existing social networks. When our mind and worldview is expanded to see His operation as always relational, we can be positioned in every situation to be of use to His plan.

Meeting in a building does not define the Ekklesia. It is relationships, which connect us together in God's plan. Whether we are led by the Spirit to meet in a house, a theater, a coffee shop, a cathedral, or in the woods does not matter. We are not identified in the Spirit by a location. We are the Ekklesia of Christ and His Body. He lives in and through us and we walk out His plan together. Where and how we meet is not as important as how we live and how Christ is expressed through one another in the Spirit.

Cracked Eikons

"Then God said, "Let us make man in our image, after our likeness. And let them have dominion over the fish of the sea and over the birds of the heavens and over the livestock and over all the earth and over every creeping thing that creeps on the earth." **Genesis 1:26**

God had a plan before the foundation of the world. By starting with this dynamic we find that the salvation of men through the cross is necessary in order to restore us to the plan of God's eternal purpose. The Godhead reveals that plan in the account of man's creation.

The Godhead's purpose is revealed in two parts. The first is for man to reflect their express image and the second is for this image to have dominion of the earth. Both these purposes were thwarted by the serpent's temptation and delayed until the Last Adam came as the express image of God and through the cross, restored dominion and authority in Heaven and in the earth in Himself.*

The power of this event is that the Community of the Godhead was expressed in the community of mankind. The serpent's temptation subsequently caused that community to be broken as both Adam and Eve became self aware through the fruit of the knowledge of good and evil. This self-focus immediately caused the image of God to be broken and the creation was cursed.

As God reveals His heart, we will know His eternal purpose. While it is true that Jesus Christ died for our sins, there is a bigger revelation that brings us into the truth. The eternal plan and purpose of God existed before the foundation of the world and before sin and the fall of man.

God's purpose is much grander than sin and individual salvation. While the redemption of man and creation is necessary, the important thing to keep in mind is that He had a plan that was in motion before the first community of mankind became self focused and experienced the knowledge of good and evil.

God originally designed our planet as a preparation ground to produce a race of beings that reflect or broadcast the eikon of God. The Hebrew word translated "image" in **Genesis 1:26-27** is tselem (צלם). In the New Testament we find the word eikon(εἰκὼν)[18] used for the word image. This is where we got the English word, "Icon." Scott McKnight of Jesus Creed coined the term "cracked eikon" in his blog.[19]

To understand the principle of an eikon, think of a computer icon. You double-click an icon to access a program on a computer. Whatever software is associated with that icon is accessed by the clicking action. What happens we people click on us?

Likewise, we are going to reflect the frequency of whichever spirit we are tuned into. **James 3:17** describes two frequencies of wisdom. One is from above and one from below. One is demonic and the other is from Heaven. Mankind became disconnected from God's frequency by Adam's disobedience and began reflecting a distorted image.

Here are a series of Scriptures from Genesis detailing the conversation of the Godhead and the response of those they created to be in their image and likeness:

> *"Then God said, 'Let Us make man in Our image,*
> *according to Our likeness; and let them rule over*
> *the fish of the sea and over the birds of the sky*
> *and over the cattle and over all the earth, and over*
> *every creeping thing that creeps on the earth.' And*

God created man in His own image, in the image of God He created him; male and female He created them." **Genesis 1:26-27**

"And the serpent said to the woman, 'You surely shall not die! For God knows that in the day you eat from it your eyes will be opened, and you will be like God, knowing good and evil.'" **Genesis 3:4-5**

"Then the LORD God said, 'Behold, the man has become like one of Us, knowing good and evil; and now, he might stretch out his hand, and take also from the tree of life, and eat, and live forever'" **Genesis 3:22**

God created the first Adam from the dust and breathed life into him through the Spirit. This Adam was created in the image of God. He was born from DNA that came from God.

The serpent was the first time we get a view of how Satan (the accuser) operates. His offer to Eve was very unusual in that the intention of the Godhead was to create man in their image and likeness. Apparently Adam and Eve did not understand what it meant to be like God because the serpent's offer was to be like God. They had either not yet been through the process of being made in God's likeness or did not understand it.

Adam allowed an infection of evil to enter into his life and into his DNA. This is often referred to as original sin. Keep in mind however, that this original sin was committed in Heaven by Lucifer (Satan's name in Heaven). He took this infection with him when he was cast out. This infection altered the DNA of the first man and he became a reflection of self rather the community of God. His nature was changed to one of self-orientation and so was the nature of his offspring. This passed onto us the "I" principle as the core of our basic personality.

God's Eternal Purpose

To grasp the power of God's original purpose for man we must start at the very beginning when the Godhead created man. These can be addressed by answering a few basic questions about life:

Why did God create us?

For what purpose am I specifically created?

How do we get on track?

Created By A Committee

"Let Us make man in Our image . . ."

This Scripture is a wonderful internal dialogue of the Godhead. How thrilling is this? The key to understanding this intimate conversation is that the Holy Spirit uses the terms, "Let Us" and "Our image." The Creators were talking as a community.**

This is a sneak preview of the eternal councils of the Godhead. Here is the first mention of the Father showing the Son what He is doing and the Son following it through. We can see the Holy Spirit was present as well as He is mentioned right at the beginning. This was a community meeting of the Godhead as they decided to create a creature called man (adam). It was further decided that this man would be created in their image and in their likeness as a community. Eve was already in Adam and they brought her out later. This obviously refutes the idea that creation of man and evolution could possibly be considered complementary explanations of our origin.

The Likeness of God

What does it mean to be an eikon of God or to be like Him and what went wrong exactly?

> *"For God knows that in the day you eat from it your eyes will be opened, and you will be like God, knowing good and evil."*
> **Genesis 3:5**

If Eve was already made in the image of God, why was the temptation to be like God so powerful and why did she want that exactly? How can we be like God if He is Spirit? Man was made a physical being, but when God breathed His Spirit into his body, he then had a spirit of his own and became a living soul. The body is only a container. The real man is on the inside.

If Adam and Eve already had a spirit, weren't they already like God? When the Holy Spirit recorded the creation of man, He intentionally let us see the conversation among the Godhead. This is one of a few instances He allows us into their amazing conversation. This is very important because it closely ties the creation of man to the three-in-one community of the Godhead: Father, Son, and Holy Spirit. Since God is community, it takes community to fellowship according to Their design.

> *"And God (Elohiym - The plural name for God)[20] created man in His own image, in the image of God He created him, male and female He created them."* **Genesis 1:27**

This record of creation is very interesting in that Adam was created first. Eve came out from a bone in his side and from them the rest of humanity was born. This was a corporate image being created through the first Adam. When he was put to sleep and God cut eve out of his side, this was a picture of things to come.

The Convergence

The work of the Last Adam was already completed on the cross when His side was pierced and blood and water proceeded from His side. This was a plan for the new humanity coming forward from within Him. Just as we are all created to be a community in Adam, we were created in Jesus with the same intention.

Man was created in the image of a God who is by nature an eternal community. The Godhead has been in fellowship for an eternity and man was created in the same image. The serpent's offer was for Eve to be like God. The truth was that Adam and Eve together were like God. It was in becoming self aware that they lost the gift of community.

Let's take hold of the precious gift of the Holy Spirit and apprehend our oneness by faith. God will work out His eternal purpose to dwell among us and to make known His manifold wisdom to principalities and powers.

One Anothering

Ἀλλήλων - allēlōn - One Another

> "From Jesus the whole body, joined and held together by every supporting ligament, grows and builds itself up in love, as each part does its work" **Ephesians 4:16**

The most often used title for ministers in the New Testament is the Greek word: allēlōn. It means One Another. **The most important minister in the Body of Christ is each one of us.**

God has placed within us the power of the universe. The same power that raised Jesus Christ from the dead now works in us.

> *"And let us consider one another in order to stir up love and good works, not forsaking the assembling of ourselves together, as is the manner of some, but exhorting one another, and so much the more as you see the Day approaching."* **Hebrews 10:24-25**

We are each qualified and expected to minister to one another. The admonition to the Hebrews to assemble is not telling us to attend worship services. Worship services are great! **The context of this Scripture, however, is for us to connect with one another daily to encourage and strengthen one another to stir up good works.** We are stirring up what is already in us.

When the Lord introduced the concept of His Ekklesia. It was both as a family and a governing body. If someone is in error and needs correction, He did not say take him or her to leaders or "the pastor." He said to bring them to the Ekklesia.

The one another's are the local ekklesia moving together in family business and governmental spiritual issues.

'"Moreover if your brother sins against you, go and tell him his fault between you and him alone. If he hears you, you have gained your brother. But if he will not hear, take with you one or two more, that 'by the mouth of two or three witnesses every word may be established.' And if he refuses to hear them, tell it to the church. But if he refuses even to hear the church, let him be to you like a heathen and a tax collector.'

'Assuredly, I say to you, whatever you bind on earth will be bound in heaven, and whatever you loose on earth will be loosed in heaven.'

'Again I say to you that if two of you agree on earth concerning anything that they ask, it will be done for them by My Father in heaven. For where two or three are gathered together in My name, I am there in the midst of them.'"
Matthew 18:15-21

When there are two or more of us gathered, we are in a place of spiritual authority. This is the reason we need to be careful what we agree upon. If we are complaining together about our problems, then we can be sure they are going to stay as problems. If we are gathering to seek the Lord's mind and pray His will into the matter, we can be sure His power will manifest supernatural results.

God has ordained relationships and is drawing us together according to His plan for our lives and ministry for one another. We could turn one another into a verb so it will have context for our daily lives. We can call it "one anothering."

We can call the following a how-to list for "one anothering." The most used reference in the list is "love one another." This list demonstrates how powerful and important our ministry to one another is in accomplishing God's eternal purpose.

One Another Patterns In Scripture

Matthew 22:35-40 — Love one another.

Matthew 18:15-19 — Restore one another.

Matthew 23:23-26 — Practice justice, mercy, and faithfulness with one another.

Matthew 28:18-20 — Disciple one another.

Mark 9:50 — Be at peace with one another.

Luke 10:25-37 — Love one another.

John 13:14 — Serve one another.

John 13:34-35 — Love one another.

John 15:12-13, 17 — Love one another.

John 17:20-26 — United with one another.

Acts 2:42-47 — Learn, share, and worship with one another.

Acts 4:32-37 — United in heart with one another.

Acts 6:1-7 — Care for one another.

Acts 11:22-26 — Encourage one another.

Romans 1:11-12 — Mutually encourage one another.

Romans 12:3-8 — Members one of another.

Romans 12:10 — Devoted to one another in brotherly love.

Romans 12:10 — Honor one another.

Romans 12:15 — Rejoice with one another.

Romans 12:15 — Weep with one another.

Romans 12:16 — Live in harmony with one another.

Romans 13:8-10 — Love one another.

Romans 14:13 — Stop passing judgment on one another.

The Convergence

Romans 14:19—Edify one another.

Romans 15:1—Bear with one another.

Romans 15:2—Please one another.

Romans 15:2—Build up one another.

Romans 15:5—United with one another.

Romans 15:7—Accept one another.

Romans 15:14—Instruct one another.

Romans 16:16—Greet one another with a holy kiss.

1 Corinthians 1:10—Agree with one another.

1 Corinthians 4:6—Do not take pride in one person over another.

1 Corinthians 10:24—Seek the good of one another.

1 Corinthians 12:4-27—Members one of another.

1 Corinthians 12:25—Equal concern for one another.

1 Corinthians 12:26—Suffer with one another.

1 Corinthians 12:26—Rejoice with one another.

1 Corinthians 13:1-8—Love one another.

1 Corinthians 14:1-3—Strengthen, encourage, and comfort one another.

1 Corinthians 16:20—Greet one another with a holy kiss.

2 Corinthians 1:3-11—Comfort one another.

2 Corinthians 2:7-11—Forgive one another and reaffirm your love for one another.

2 Corinthians 5:14-21—Live for one another.

2 Corinthians 13:12—Greet one another with a holy kiss.

Galatians 5:13—Serve one another in love.

Galatians 5:15—Stop biting and devouring one another.

Galatians 5:26—Stop provoking and envying one another.

Galatians 6:1-3—Restore one another.

Galatians 6:1-3—Carry each other's burdens.

Ephesians 4:1-7—Bear with one another in love.

Ephesians 4:11-16—Equip one another through speaking the truth in love.

Ephesians 4:25—Speak truthfully to one another.

Ephesians 4:29—Speak words that build up one another.

Ephesians 4:32—Be kind and compassionate to one another.

Ephesians 4:32—Forgive each other.

Ephesians 5:19—Speak to one another in psalms, hymns, and spiritual songs.

Ephesians 5:21—Submit to one another.

Philippians 2:1-5—Consider others better than self.

Philippians 2:1-5—Look out for the interests of others.

Philippians 4:2—Agree with each other in the Lord.

Colossians 1:25-2:2—Admonish, and teach one another.

Colossians 3:9—Do not lie to one another.

Colossians 3:12-14—Bear with one another.

Colossians 3:12-14—Forgive one another.

Colossians 3:15-17—Teach and admonish one another with all wisdom.

1 Thessalonians 2:12—Encourage, comfort, and urge one another.

1 Thessalonians 3:12—Increase in overflowing love for one another.

1 Thessalonians 4:9—Love each other.

1 Thessalonians 4:18—Encourage each other.

1 Thessalonians 5:11—Encourage one another.

1 Thessalonians 5:11—Build up each other.

1 Thessalonians 5:13—Live in peace with one another.

1 Thessalonians 5:14—Urge, warn, encourage, help, and be patient with one another.

1 Thessalonians 5:15—Be kind to each other.

2 Thessalonians 1:3—Love one another.

2 Thessalonians 3:15—Warn one another as brothers.

1 Timothy 5:20—Rebuke one another.

2 Timothy 2:2—Disciple and teach one another.

2 Timothy 2:22-26—Gently instruct one another in kindness.

2 Timothy 3:16-17—Teach, rebuke, correct, and train one another.

2 Timothy 4:1-8—Preach, correct, rebuke, encourage, and carefully instruct one another.

Titus 1:6-11—Encourage one another by sound doctrine.

Titus 2:1-15—Mentor one another.

Hebrews 3:7-19—Encourage one another daily.

Hebrews 10:24—Consider how to spur one another on toward love and good deeds.

Hebrews 10:25—Do not give up meeting with one another.

Hebrews 10:25—Encourage one another.

Hebrews 13:1—Keep on loving each other as brothers.

James 2:8—Love one another.

James 4:11—Do not slander one another.

James 5:9—Do not grumble against one another.

James 5:13-16—Pray for one another.

Convergence – Summing Up All Things In Christ

James 5:16—Confess your sins to one another.

1 Peter 1:22—Love one another deeply from the heart.

1 Peter 3:8—Live in harmony with one another.

1 Peter 4:8—Above all, love each other deeply.

1 Peter 4:9—Offer hospitality to one another without grumbling.

1 Peter 4:10—Use all gifts to serve one another faithfully.

1 Peter 5:5—Clothe yourselves with humility toward one another.

1 Peter 5:14—Greet one another with a kiss of love.

1 John 1:7—Have fellowship with one another.

1 John 2:7-17—Love one another.

1 John 3:11-15—Love one another.

1 John 3:16-18—Lay down your life for one another.

1 John 4:7-21—Love one another.

2 John 5—Love one another.

Kingdom Hospitality

Our homes are a lighthouse to the community. Our lives and daily rhythms are platforms of ministry in which we represent the interests of Heaven. There is a powerful supernatural blessing built into simple hospitality. It is so significant that Jesus said in His famous Matthew 25 account that He would separate the sheep and the goats at the final judgment based on hospitality. The sheep ministered to the basic needs of others and the goats did not. Hospitality is therefore, a visible and measurable fruit of righteousness.

This particular ministry is often overlooked and quite challenging to the western mindset. The nuclear family was made popular during the industrial revolution and was eventually perpetuated through consumer advertising. Prior to this, extended generation families were the norm. The nuclear family perpetuated an isolated private lifestyle that was separate from extended family and church. The church building became a neutral ground and platform for ministry and the home was a private place not offered for ministry to others.

There is a supernatural dimension to hospitality. Our homes should not be a refuge, but rather presented to Christ as a platform of ministry. Personal boundaries are not found in the New Testament examples of the first century believers. Just the opposite is actually the norm.

When we open our homes to others, it becomes a place of accountability rather than a secret place to harbor our personal issues. This also empowers us by breaking the stronghold in which we believe we have a right to our "private lives."

When we minister to the most basic needs of others, we are

exerting our kingly authority and following the example of Jesus Christ. When we open our lives and homes to serve the inhabitants of this planet, we are also living out our function as ambassadors of Christ. The home is one of the primary vehicles used in the first century to spread the gospel. It was always a place of teaching, prayer, prophetic power and fellowship.

Somehow, the service of others has a very powerful affect on both angels and the Lord Himself. Jesus said that what we do to the least, we are really doing to Him. He is the final recipient of our hospitality.

In Genesis 18, here is an amazing account of Abraham ministering hospitality to three strangers that came to his tent. It appears that he was entertaining two angels and the Lord.

Ministering To Angels

"Do not forget to entertain strangers, for by so doing some have unwittingly entertained angels." **Hebrews 13:2**

Ministering To God

"'When the Son of Man comes in His glory, and all the holy angels with Him, then He will sit on the throne of His glory. All the nations will be gathered before Him, and He will separate them one from another, as a shepherd divides his sheep from the goats. And He will set the sheep on His right hand, but the goats on the left. Then the King will say to those on His right hand, 'Come, you blessed of My Father, inherit the kingdom prepared for you from the foundation of the world: for I was hungry and you gave Me food; I was thirsty and you gave Me drink; I was a stranger and you took Me in; I was naked and you clothed Me; I was sick and you visited Me; I was in prison and you came to Me.

Then the righteous will answer Him, saying, 'Lord, when did we see You hungry and feed You, or thirsty and give You drink? When did we see You a stranger and take You in, or naked and clothe You? Or when did we see You sick, or in prison, and come to You?' And the King will answer and say to them, 'Assuredly, I say to you, inasmuch as you did it to one of the least of these My brethren, you did it to Me.

Then He will also say to those on the left hand, 'Depart from Me, you cursed, into the everlasting fire prepared for the devil and his angels: for I was hungry and you gave Me no food; I was thirsty and you gave Me no drink; I was a stranger and you did not take Me in, naked and you did not clothe Me, sick and in prison and you did not visit Me.'

Then they also will answer Him, saying, 'Lord, when did we see You hungry or thirsty or a stranger or naked or sick or in prison, and did not minister to You?' Then He will answer them, saying, 'Assuredly, I say to you, inasmuch as you did not do it to one of the least of these, you did not do it to Me. And these will go away into everlasting punishment, but the righteous into eternal life.'" **Matthew 25:31-46**

Meeting the simple needs of others touches the Lord Jesus directly. If you ever feel that you cannot be of service, remember there are 7 billion people in the world. Jesus directly receives what we do to the least as if it were being done to Him personally. This applies to the good and the bad we may do to others.

The 99% principle applies here. If you can't get a shot at singing at the local worship services, don't sweat it. There are innumerable ways to change the world and minister to Jesus through others. In the 99% ministry, there is never a line to wait in or someone trying to tell you that, "You are not ready." There is enough for everyone to do and the Lord has told us we need more laborers in the harvest.

Chapter Two

THE SPIRIT OF LIFE

"There is therefore now no condemnation to those who are in Christ Jesus, who do not walk according to the flesh, but according to the Spirit. For the law of the Spirit of life in Christ Jesus has made me free from the law of sin and death."
Romans 8:1-2

"If then you were raised with Christ, seek those things which are above, where Christ is, sitting at the right hand of God. Set your mind on things above, not on things on the earth. For you died, and your life is hidden with Christ in God. When Christ who is our life appears, then you also will appear with Him in glory." *Colossians 3:1-4*

"To them God willed to make known what are the riches of the glory of this mystery among the Gentiles: which is Christ in you, the hope of glory." *Colossians 1:27*

Hamartia Principle

There is a principle at work in the world that is so powerful that affects us each at the very core of our identity and being. Its name is Sin. Sin in the singular sense is different from the plural idea of our sinful behaviors.

Romans 5 demonstrates to us that we are not sinners because we sin, but rather we sin because we are already sinners by birth. Sin is expressed in the original Greek as "Hamartia." A simple word study on Hamartia reveals that this word was originally used in terms of archery. It was used to relate the missing of a target by an archer's arrow. A slave would stand under the target in a hole and when the archer missed the target he would yell out, "HAMARTIA."

Our personality is formed with the Sin Principle at the core of our identity. The world is under the sway of the wicked one and it is through the law of sin that he holds us captive. The devil is quite aware of sin's power because he too is a slave to sin. That is why he has no hope of redemption. It is through the power of Sin or the Hamartia Principle that Satan controls the world and tempts us to sin.

Whenever the Scripture speaks of God forgiving sin, the Holy Spirit always refers to "sins," because forgiveness relates to our behavior. The sin nature in us cannot be forgiven and never receives forgiveness. That is where death is the only possible solution. God therefore does not forgive Sin, but only sins. Scripture tells us to, "confess our sins" (**1 John 1:9).** The Old Testament only addressed sin in a general sense. The New Testament, however, brings a new understanding. It is in the revelation of Jesus Christ that we begin to see that Sin has its own identity and is a major character in the story of our lives and has a major place in the operation of the world in general.

While the original sin of pride was committed in Heaven by Lucifer, Sin is actually a force and power that entered into the world through Adam. Its power is so great that even Satan is only a prince as he too bows his knee to the power of Sin. We are each born into captivity in this world and Sin is our master.

This is how the Holy Spirit wants us to understand Sin. In **Romans 3:23** He tells us that, "all have fallen short of the glory of God." This illustrates that the target is God's glory and that hamartia or sin is missing this target.

The issue is God's glory. Our whole life is to be measured by the glory. This is not a goal, but a living process as God works the life of Christ among us.

The result will be our transformation together as this same glory transforms us into the image of Christ. When we pursue His glory, our transformation is assured. Most of the adversary's activity is to keep us distracted from this valuable life giving process.

If we are not hitting the mark, we are in the realm of death. There is no neutral ground. We are either drawing from the indwelling Christ as our life or the law of sin and death is working its death power in our lives.

Paul's Letter to the Roman Ekklesia reveals the Hamartia Principle to a great degree. It could also be called the Law of Sin and Death. Romans 6-8 is a power packed how-to for recognizing the power of sin and activating the Spirit of Life in Christ Jesus. **1 Corinthians 15:56** tells us, "The sting of death is sin." Therefore, the opposite of sin is life.

Activating ZOE
The Law of The Spirit of Life

Romans 8:2 powerfully reveals to us, "the Spirit of Life in Christ Jesus delivers us from the Law of Sin and Death." There are some very specific principles involved here that are life and death matters. We must take certain actions to activate the Law of Life.

> *"I will give you a new heart and put a new spirit within you; I will take the heart of stone out of your flesh and give you a heart of flesh. I will put My Spirit within you and cause you to walk in My statutes, and you will keep My judgments and do them."* **Ezekiel 36:26-37**

ZOE Defined

The new Covenant has several components. A valuable dynamic of the Covenant is that we receive an entirely new spirit. This is the key to activating the law of The Spirit of Life. Just as we have a stomach that processes food, our newly received spirit is an organ within us that processes and distributes the higher life form of God within and through us.

The stomach in our flesh has a powerful influence over our spiritual heritage. Esau sold his inheritance for a bowl of soup[21] and Adam and Eve both sold their access to the tree of life for some knowledge fruit.[22] The new spirit as a stomach is a powerful parallel.

A monkey can pretend to be human, but would require a supernatural recreation to actually become a human, just as we cannot live the Christ life as a human being with our natural human life. God is a higher life form. The life of the Spirit is called ζωή (ZOE)[23] in the original Greek. We now have access and the spiritual ability to draw upon ZOE. Our new spirit is the organ God gives us to interact with the Spirit of Life and process this God Life into our human experience. It is a mingling of our spirit and His Spirit that causes us to the live the Christ life.

Remember, the Tree of Life from the garden in Eden? Life is to be consumed and processed in and through us.

The ZOE is the power and force behind the mystery of God that has been hidden for all the ages.

> *"the mystery which has been hidden from ages and from generations, but now has been revealed to His saints. To them God willed to make known what are the riches of the glory of this mystery among the Gentiles: which is Christ in you, the hope of glory."* **Colossians 1:26-27**

The transformation that God is working in us works through a process. Conforming us to the image of God is not a goal, but a process. It is a spiritually organic process that is worked in and through us as we consume God with our spirit and His life is distributed to our mind and body.

We are the Body of Christ and ZOE nourishes us as living organisms. God distributes ZOE to us though the spoken Word. We then, as a living Body, supply one another by what every joint and ligament supplies.[24]

"Man shall not live by bread alone, but by every word that comes from the mouth of God." **Matthew 4:4**

Living is not something we exercise as a conscious effort. We live and breathe as part of a natural system God put in place in our physical bodies. We breathe in the air that gives us life every second without a thought. The common practice in the West is to smack a baby's bottom to activate the first breath at birth. It is quite possible some of us have never had our spiritual bottoms smacked to activate the Law of Life in us. It is God's will for us to draw upon ZOE in the same way as we breathe air. His Divine Life is to infuse our thoughts and to quicken our mortal bodies. We are to be so immersed in His ZOE that there is overflow to the world around us bringing Christ (The Anointing) into every atmosphere.

There are natural and spiritual laws that order the physical and spiritual universe around us. Many of them are constant and predictable which allows us to tap into natural forces of energy and create technologies to capture or release their expected results.

For example, the law of gravity has a principle in which helium is lighter than air. We can believe this all day and get no benefit. However, if we act on this knowledge and fill a balloon with helium and seal it, we can activate the law of gravity. The balloon will rise in harmony with our act of faith.

Activating The Law of The Spirit of Life

There are in the same way, specific actions revealed in Scripture that will align and position us to benefit and release the power of spiritual laws. We are going to look at the power of activating the Law of the Spirit of Life in Christ Jesus. Once we activate this law and principle within us, we will accelerate the process of spiritual growth as we facilitate our spirit to process the Spirit of Life.

The origin of Sin/Hamartia is one of the keys to understanding its power over us. Satan was originally a very powerful cherubim named Lucifer in the Temple of Heaven. He was a covering cherub and he stood directly between God and those who worshiped. We could say he was a steward of the glory. The problem began when he began to want things for himself. He began to trade on his access to the revelation. Paul warned about the pride that could result in an abundance of heavenly revelations in his testimony about seeing the third heaven in **2 Corinthians 12:2-8**.

The original sin was when he began to move into the "I" realm of selfish awareness and ambition. The infection started here with the famous five "I Will's" of **Isaiah 14:**

>   **"I will ascend into heaven;"**

>   **"I will exalt my throne above the stars of God;"**

>   **"I will also sit on the mount of the congregation;"**

>   **"I will ascend above the heights of the clouds,"**

>   **"I will be like the Most High;"**

God's eternal purpose as revealed in Genesis is to form man in the image of the Godhead. The Father, Son and Holy Spirit form a divine community that has always existed in perfect communication and harmony. It was their intention to create mankind as a community.

The serpent tempted Eve with an offer to be "like" God. If they were created in their image and likeness, why was this even a topic of discussion? The offer was to be "like" God as an individual. The goal and result was independence.

The moment both Adam and Eve chose knowledge over life; they were infected with the Hamartia Principle. They became self aware, disconnected from the tree of life, and the "I" was created.

In the Greek Scriptures, the flesh is referred to as σάρξ - **(SARX)**.[25] This sarx or flesh is actually the "I" that was created in mankind through Adam's disobedience. This is passed to each of us in our DNA at conception. There is no fixing this sarx. Our personality is formed with selfishness at its root. It is at the core of who we are and the only possible way to deal with the self/sarx is death.

There is a wealth of powerful elements released to us through the finished work of Jesus Christ. **The blood was shed for God.** His justice was fulfilled. It released the sin remission and cleansing power. The blood cleanses our conscience and **Hebrews 9:23** tells us that the blood cleansed the Heavenly Temple. This was possibly the cleansing from the original sin of Lucifer. **The cross however, was for us.** The death of Christ was also our death. This is the core power of the message of the cross. **The "I" principle in me died with Christ.**

> *"I have been crucified with Christ; it is no longer I who live, but Christ lives in me; and the life which I now live in the flesh I live by faith in the Son of God, who loved me and gave Himself for me."* **Galatians 2:20**

We could also say it is no longer my life to live, but the ZOE of God is my source. The way to activate this life is revealed as faith. We simply receive this ZOE as our life just as we breathe in air. Christ in us is our source.

> *"What shall we say then? Shall we continue in sin that grace may abound? Certainly not! How shall we who died to sin live any longer in it? Or do you not know that as many of us as were baptized into Christ Jesus were baptized into His death? Therefore we were buried with Him through baptism into death, that just as Christ was raised from the dead by the glory of the Father, even so we also should walk in newness of life. For if we have been united together in the likeness of His death, certainly we also shall be in the likeness of His*

*resurrection, **knowing this, that our old man was crucified with Him, that the body of sin might be done away with**, that we should no longer be slaves of sin. For he who has died has been freed from sin. Now if we died with Christ, we believe that we shall also live with Him, knowing that Christ, having been raised from the dead, dies no more. Death no longer has dominion over Him. For the death that He died, He died to sin once for all; but the life that He lives, He lives to God. Likewise you also, **reckon yourselves to be dead indeed to sin, but alive to God in Christ Jesus our Lord**. Therefore do not let sin reign in your mortal body, that you should obey it in its lusts. And do not present your members as instruments of unrighteousness to sin, but **present yourselves to God as being alive from the dead, and your members as instruments of righteousness to God**. For (hamartia) sin shall not have dominion over you, for you are not under law but under grace."* **Romans 6: 1-14**

There are two keys to activating the ZOE found in **Romans 6:**

1. The first is to reckon our "self" dead. That is an accounting word. If we have $5 in our pocket, we can reckon that it is true. The same holds true for us having died with Christ.

2. The second key is to present ourselves alive in Christ and to present our members as instruments of righteousness. This could be broken down by saying, "I give you my thoughts, feelings, attitudes, etc..."

As we draw upon Him, the Spirit of Life infuses every part of our being with ZOE. He quickens our mind and mortal body and He makes our emotions become supernatural portals revealing the fruit of the Spirit.

"But the fruit of the Spirit is love, joy, peace, longsuffering, kindness, goodness, faithfulness, gentleness, self-control. Against such there is no law." **Galatians 5:22**

The Anointing

The anointing can be defined as, "God empowering the flesh to do the impossible." or "What is impossible for man is possible for God."

From a New Testament perspective, we could even say that the anointing of God is His glory in earthen vessels.[26]

The meaning of the word "anoint" is "to pour on, smear all over or rub into." In the Old Testament, someone who was anointed by God for special service to God had oil poured or smeared on him. When Samuel anointed David to be King it was because God chose him.[27]

> *"The Spirit of the Lord is upon Me, because He has anointed Me To preach the gospel to the poor..."* **Luke 4:18**

The anointing is not the Spirit Himself, but His power. Jesus said the Spirit of the Lord was upon Him because of the anointing. To be anointed by God is not only to be chosen, but also to be empowered by Him for the task or position to which He has called you. The Hebrew word "Messiah" and the Greek word "Christ" both mean "the Anointed."

What was the assignment given to Jesus?

> *"To preach the gospel to the poor...heal the brokenhearted...preach deliverance to the captives, and recovering of sight to the blind...set at liberty them that are bruised..."* **Luke 4:18-19**

News of the Anointed and His Anointing was the "good news" or "gospel" the first century believers delivered. When Peter was directed to preach the gospel to the Gentiles for the very first time, he told them:

Convergence – Summing Up All Things In Christ

"How God anointed Jesus of Nazareth with the Holy Ghost and with power: who went about doing good, and healing all that were oppressed of the devil; for God was with him"
Acts 10:38-39

When the poor and brokenhearted hear the message, the anointing brings the power. The Anointed One and His Anointing come to destroy the yokes from their backs.

God is still confirming the ministry of Jesus Christ. It is still His mission, His anointing, and His desire to destroy the yokes. We are His Body and He is still doing the same mission through us.

If you are in Christ, you are in the Anointed One and The Anointed One is in you. He is The Christ! He is not Mr. Christ. It is not a name, but a function.

Despite common practice, there is no reference to any type of teaching anointing in the New Testament. God has placed the power to learn in each of us. We don't need a central teacher because there is learning anointing in us and we all have it! We all can be a teacher because the learning comes from within us.

"But the anointing which you have received from Him abides in you, and you do not need that anyone teach you; but as the same anointing teaches you concerning all things, and is true, and is not a lie, and just as it has taught you, you will abide in Him." **1 John 2:27**

The key is that one cannot separate the Anointed One and the anointing. If you're in the Anointed One, then you're in the anointing. It's a package deal.

Each time Christ is used in the New Testament read it to say, "The Anointed and His Anointing." We are the Body of The Anointed One and we have His anointing. We embody His anointing.

There is one anointing because we are embodying the Anointed One. Why would we settle for some special sub-anointing when we have the Anointed One Himself dwelling in us and filling our lives with power?

Weakness Is The Doorway To Anointing

The key to moving in the power of the Christ was spoken to Paul by the Lord Jesus:

> *"And He said to me, 'My grace is sufficient for you, for My strength is made perfect in weakness.' Therefore most gladly I will rather boast in my infirmities, that the power of Christ may rest upon me. Therefore I take pleasure in infirmities, in reproaches, in needs, in persecutions, in distresses, for Christ's sake. For when I am weak, then I am strong."*
> **2 Corinthians 12:9-12**

It is not human giftedness that we need. It is in our weakness that the Christ with His anointing and power rises from within us and upon our flesh to accomplish the impossible. The power of the Anointed One rests upon our weakness!

> *"Now to Him who is able to do exceedingly abundantly above all that we ask or think, according to the power that works in us, to Him be glory in the church by Christ Jesus to all generations, forever and ever. Amen."* **Ephesians 3:20**

On the other side of the issue is the antichrist or false Christ. The antichrist is not a non-Christ, but a false one. A false anointed one is someone counterfeiting the true Anointed One. This could produce "false signs and wonders."

We share in Christ's anointing. He has one anointing and it is distributed to His body. Just as the Ekklesia and Christ are one, so is His anointing.

Convergence – Summing Up All Things In Christ

And Jesus answered and said to them: "Take heed that no one deceives you. For many will come in My name, saying, 'I am the Christ,' and will deceive many." Matthew 24:4-5

If someone is running around saying that they are Jesus, people will think they are a crackpot. There are, however, plenty of people running around saying they are, "The Anointed One" or even that they have more anointing or a specialized anointing.

"Little children, it is the last hour; and as you have heard that the Antichrist is coming, even now many antichrists have come, by which we know that it is the last hour." 1 John 2:18

Do not be deceived by the antichrist spirit and seek any form of power that is not directly being released by the Lord Jesus Christ. His power is not for sale, does not enhance our strengths, and only brings glory to God in Christ. No flesh will glory when God's true anointed power is manifested. That means the "I" principle and people's ambitious egos will be shown for what they truly represent.

Remember, there is one Anointed One: the Christ. We are all partakers of His anointing as we abide in Him. This is not something He delegates or gives us to handle in His absence. He distributes His anointing through us as we abide in Him. This means we must be plugged into Christ in order to draw upon His power. This is what **Romans 8:5** and **Colossians 3:1** refers to as setting our mind to the Spirit and **James 3:17** calls the wisdom or frequency from above.

When we are tuned into the Spirit and living as spiritually minded, He infuses us with a constant overflow of life and power. When we unplug with carnal or natural thinking, it brings death. We are in Christ, the Anointed One and the same power that works in and through Him works in and through us, His Body.

Knowing God's Will

ὑπόστασις (NOUS)
Mind, thought, understanding, spiritual perception[29]

> *"I beseech you therefore, brethren, by the mercies of God, that you **present your bodies** a living sacrifice, holy, acceptable to God, which is your reasonable service. And do not be conformed to this world, but **be transformed by the renewing of your mind, that you may prove what is that good and acceptable and perfect will of God.** "* **Romans 12:1-3**

It is God's intention that we know His will. When we present our bodies to Him as a living sacrifice, we come into the glorious work of our High Priest as He works a transformation in us by dividing our soul and spirit.[30] This work occurs not just in our mind, but also at the very core of being, or the nous.

This is similar to presenting our members as instruments of righteousness as illustrated in Romans 6.

> *"And do not present your members as instruments of unrighteousness to sin, but present yourselves to God as being alive from the dead, and your members as instruments of righteousness to God."* **Romans 6:13**

The Greek word for transformed is where we get the word metamorphosis: **μεταμορφόω (Metamorphoo)**[31] This is what happens when a caterpillar goes into a cocoon and is shifted in its DNA to become a butterfly. The inward work of God on our nous is so dramatic that when we present our bodies, or DNA to God, we are so changed that we not only know His good, acceptable and perfect will, but His will becomes our identity at the core of our being. We become God's perfect will.

This concerns more than simply doing the will of God. Our core identity is being aligned with the perfect will of God and our behavior is the result of our being conformed to the image of Christ. We move into the power of being rather than doing.

The word 'metamorphoo' is only used three times in Scripture. It is also used in **2 Corinthians 3:18** to explain the metamorphosis from a different view. Here, The Holy Spirit explains that a veil is being taken away from our hearts. He says that, "As we behold the glory of the Lord without the veil in front of our faces, we behold the glory of the Lord as in a mirror, and we are transfigured [metamorphoo] into the same image from glory to glory."

The third time the Holy Spirit uses this word, 'metamorphoo', is in the **Matthew Chapter 17** account of the transfiguration of Jesus. This renewing of our minds is the power of God transfiguring us into the glory of Jesus Christ in our hearts.

The transformation of our nous will bring us into an inward "knowing" of God's good acceptable, and perfect will. The Holy Spirit is transforming us so powerfully that our very DNA is aligning with the perfect will of God.

God is working all things together in the universe for the purpose of this inward transfiguration. The power of this principle lies not in the plural tense, **"present your bodies as a living sacrifice."** This is true community worship in action. We can also apply some practical principles to assist us in discerning His direction.

The principle of first mention means that the first time something is mentioned in Scripture contains within it a secret to understanding the principle. The first time that worship was mentioned was in the **Genesis 22** account of Abraham taking his son up on the mountain to worship. He did bow down when he met the two angels and the Lord at his tent. The second account using the same word is translated as worship. The Hebrew word used was: "shachah" which means to bow down. This instance, however, was the sacrifice of his son Isaac. So worship and sacrifice are closely tied by the nature of this first mention.

The community dynamic is the real power of this principle. When we collectively offer our bodies as a living sacrifice, we position ourselves for transformation as member of His Body and not individuals. We are glorified together in Christ.

Four principles we can apply to discern God's will:

1. **Events** - We can see and understand that He is working all things according to His purpose in our lives. Sometimes events are occurring to lead us to a place of needed revelation.

2. **Guidance - Romans 8:14** – "For as many as are led by the Spirit of God, these are sons of God." The inward witness and communication of the Spirit of Life.

3. **Scripture -** If the first two items align with Scripture we can be quite sure we are on track to God's will. The Scriptures offer us the exact and express will of God and will always afford us an absolute measurement to harmonize our lives with the Body of Christ.

4. **Community -** God speaks through the Body of Christ and community. We are empowered by the community of God and submitting ourselves to one another ensures we are free of self-deception.

Dividing Soul & Spirit

Most often discipleship is approached from an extraction viewpoint in which we extract people from their lives into a neutral classroom setting. The purpose is to instruct them with information.

The academic or instructional approach to discipleship is considerably different than the approach taken by our Lord Jesus and the first century believers. If we want to experience the exponential growth and multiplication of the Body of Christ that prevailed in the first century, we can by simply drawing on their example.

There is an important distinction between the Bible and the Living Word. Missing this distinction has made discipleship and Bible study into an academic exercise. Being discipled by the Living Word is more amazing and intrusive than programs or studies could ever accomplish.

Jesus Christ is The Word of God. In the Greek language, this is expressed by the word **"LOGOS."** Because the English language is not as robust and descriptive as the original Scripture, we often miss the full context of what was being expressed by the Holy Spirit. For example, the Word made flesh is again the **"LOGOS"** and the spoken word of God is expressed in Greek by the word, **"RHEMA."**

The identity of the Word of God

1. **John 1:1-3** - In the beginning was the Word, and the Word was with God, and the Word was God. He was in the beginning with God. All things were made through Him, and without Him nothing was made that was made.

2. **1 John 5:7** - For there are three that bear witness in heaven: the Father, the Word, and the Holy Spirit; and these three are one.

3. **Revelation 19:11-13** - Now I saw heaven opened, and behold, a white horse. And He who sat on him was called Faithful and True, and in righteousness He judges and makes war. His eyes were like a flame of fire, and on His head were many crowns. He had a name written that no one knew except Himself. He was clothed with a robe dipped in blood, and His name is called The Word of God.

4. **Hebrews 4:11-14** - Let us therefore be diligent to enter that rest, lest anyone fall according to the same example of disobedience. For the Word of God is living and powerful, and sharper than any two-edged sword, piercing even to the division of soul and spirit, and of joints and marrow, and is a discerner of the thoughts and intents of the heart. And there is no creature hidden from His sight, but all things are naked and open to the eyes of Him to whom we must give account. Seeing then that we have a great High Priest who has passed through the heavens, Jesus the Son of God, let us hold fast our confession.

The Living Word is revealed as our High Priest. The entering into the rest is our partaking of the finished work of the cross and yielding ourselves to the inward work of the Living Word as He works supernatural circumcision into our hearts.

The illustration in **Hebrews 4** parallels the actual practice of our High Priest, Jesus cutting open the sacrifice to the bone with a very sharp knife. During the Old Testament period when people presented an offering, they bound their sacrifice to the altar. The priest then killed it with a sharp knife, parting it into two and piercing to the division of the joints and marrow, exposing to view all that formerly had been hidden from human sight. This would be all our old man being brought out into the light and removed from being our center of life.

In the beginning the Word of God worked in creation by separating light from darkness, so now He works within us as the Sword of the Spirit, piercing to the separation of the spirit and soul.

Our part is to present ourselves to Him as a living sacrifice, and His is to reveal the hidden intents of our hearts and let them pour out in death as He divides our soul and spirit and transforms us into His image.

This could also be viewed as His work in our hearts as we receive both a new spirit and the Holy Spirit.[28] Paul wrote a letter to the Colossians and shared an amazing account that happens in baptism:

> *"In Him you were also circumcised with the circumcision made without hands, by putting off the body of the sins of the flesh, by the circumcision of Christ, buried with Him in baptism, in which you also were raised with Him through faith in the working of God, who raised Him from the dead."*
> **Colossians 2:11-12**

The dividing of the soul and spirit also includes a breaking open of the soul. This releases our new spirit and the Holy Spirit into all areas of our being so God's life can reach us deep within and liberate us from bondage of the self. This is the circumcision of the heart made without hands.

The altar in the Old Testament speaks of the cross in the New Testament. We must first embrace our death in the cross. If we want the power of the cross to be worked in us, we must present ourselves as a living sacrifice.[29] We lay our self/soul independence on the altar and our High Priest does the cutting.

Spiritually Minded

"For to be carnally minded is death, but to be spiritually minded is life and peace." **Romans 8:6**

There is a practical application to being spiritually minded and it is an important dynamic of both disciple making and spiritual warfare.

The Great Commission of Matthew 28 Tells us that one of the components of disciple making is teaching new disciples to obey. This is also the fruit of our spiritual weapons.

"For though we walk in the flesh, we do not war according to the flesh. For the weapons of our warfare are not carnal but mighty in God for pulling down strongholds, casting down arguments and every high thing that exalts itself against the knowledge of God, bringing every thought into captivity to the obedience of Christ" **2 Corinthians 10:3-5**

Notice that this is speaking of spiritual warfare and therefore, a supernatural manifestation of God's Spirit from within. The Spirit conducts all warfare. We simply go along for the ride.

We run into the Romans 7 struggle that Paul spoke about in which all our efforts to not sin are met with failure. That is not the abundant life promised in Christ and believing in the futility of sin is the reason so many perceive themselves as defeated in the Body of Christ.

You are about to shift into the convergence flow of the Holy Spirit and bring your thoughts into the Spiritual Flow of the Spirit of Life in Christ Jesus. The next section will detail the process of coming into harmony with the Mind of Christ.

Mind of Christ
Wearing "Son Glasses"

We each have an inner dialogue or our own voice that speaks to us. This voice inside of us is the actual person inside of us. The voice is our thoughts. This is inward world is where the victory in our life is won.

Once we begin to tune into the network activity of our inner man it is time to slow it down and begin to listen. That voice that always talks inside of us needs to be harnessed and presented to the Spirit. This is going to be a game changer for you when you begin operating in this dimension.

Our minds have been programmed over our lifetime with immense amounts of identity related data. By the age of 14, a child that watches as little as 1 hour a day of television has been exposed to over 5000 hours of identity related information driven by the consumer culture (The world).

It's not a matter of whether our children are being discipled, but really the question is who is discipling them?

We pick up scripts and filters that manage the input we are receiving from the world around us as well as a pattern of thinking. This is what Scripture calls being conformed to this world.[30]

This thoughts that flow through this inner dialogue are different than our beliefs. The thoughts are filtered through our beliefs and this often will determine our behavior. When the Spirit is in charge of the thoughts, we are responding to Him. When we are in control of our thoughts we are reacting to the flesh.

This can be the result of reacting to long established scripts or "if-then" statements. Over time, we pick up behavior patterns that are virtually automatic.

An example of an "if-then statement would be something like, "If someone disrespects me, then I get angry."

A very practical way to present your thoughts to the Holy Spirit is to change the pronouns of your inner dialogue. Instead thinking to, "I" we think to the Lord. The "I" is the flesh and thinking to the flesh is enmity with God.

For example, instead of saying, "How do I feel?" or "What do I think?" Try this: "What do you feel about this Lord?" and "What is your thought on the matter?" This simple exercise can be a game changer as we begin to capture our thought flow and direct it to the inward dwelling Spirit rather than ourselves. Our thought life becomes a never ceasing prayer life.

The same principle holds true for our imagination. We must give our imagination to the Spirit for His use. The screen in our minds is similar in function to a TV screen. It is only going to broadcast the signal we are receiving. We can control this to a great degree by controlling what goes into it through our eye and ear gates.

> *"How much more shall the blood of Christ, who through the eternal Spirit offered Himself without spot to God, cleanse your conscience from dead works to serve the living God?"*
> **Hebrews 9:14**

If our memories and imagination have been polluted by the past, we can bring cleansing by presenting them to God for cleansing in the blood of Jesus. We operate from picture memories sometimes just like we do from if-then statements.

The Yetzer – Energized Imagination

There is a traditional Hebrew thought about the imagination. They call it the yetzer hara, or the inner impulse to gravitate toward selfish gratification (idolatry).

This concept first appears in Genesis 6:5 where the wickedness of man is described as "every imagination (yetzer) of the thoughts of his heart was only evil (ra)." In the New Testament, yetzer hara is called the "carnal mind," the "sin nature," or the "old man."

Yetzer is a neutral word used to refer to something formed or shaped, like pottery fashioned by the hand of a potter. Just as a potter purposes a shape before forming an object, so that which is intended within the heart will form our character.[31] The yetzer is therefore neutral. When submitted to the Spirit for His use, He can communicate amazing things to us.

When we see in the physical sense, our eyes are only operating as lenses that send a signal to our yetzer. It is here that we actually see. The same holds true for all of our senses. Our body is nothing more than an earth suit that enables us to interact with the third dimensional world around us.

Our newly acquired spirit that we receive at our new birth also gives us the ability to see and sense the spiritual realm. We must grow and mature this spirit through practice. We must develop our spiritual frame of reference. This is useful as we are now citizens of Heaven.[32]

The yetzer then becomes a gateway between both worlds. Within our natural mind we have something called a hippocampus. If we were to design a comparable computer, it would be the size of the state of Texas. While our brains are remarkable, our ability to process information is limited.

As babies we cannot, at first, see further than a few inches. We develop a frame of reference by touching, feeling and experiencing the world around us. Our brains are constantly receiving millions of perceptive inputs every minute. The hippocampus has a unique function in filtering the data against our frame of reference. If there is no frame of reference, it is discarded and we do not even notice it.

A frame of reference could also be called a paradigm or window that we filter our perceptions through. One of the things uniting believers is that we share the same center of reference in Christ. He becomes our filter.
When we become spiritually minded we begin transcending the natural limitations of our mind and Christ's mind becomes our frame of reference. We essentially begin to see the world through "Son Glasses."

When we hide Scripture in our heart, we expand our ability to see spiritually. We are constantly receiving input from the physical and spiritual realms into our yetzer. We discard much of the spiritual input because we lack a frame of reference to perceive it and through lack of experience have not exercised our spiritual senses.

> *"For though by this time you ought to be teachers, you need someone to teach you again the first principles of the oracles of God; and you have come to need milk and not solid food. For everyone who partakes only of milk is unskilled in the word of righteousness, for he is a babe. But solid food belongs to those who are of full age, that is, those who by reason of use have their senses exercised to discern both good and evil."* **Hebrews 5:12-14**

The capacity to use our yetzer as an interface from the Spirit of God allows us to walk in the power of the unseen. We simply need to exercise it and mature in this area of our spiritual growth process. We can then walk in the creative power of God and trust in what we see in the Spirit to become manifest in the physical.

A spiritually energized imagination is the key to moving in the convergence. We can see God's will even in the unpleasant circumstances and move through them with great joy. We trust that even affliction is working for us as we are processed into Christ! We can draw upon the glory in every situation.

> *"For our light affliction, which is but for a moment, is working for us a far more exceeding and eternal weight of glory, while we do not look at the things which are seen, but at the things which are not seen. For the things which are seen are temporary, but the things which are not seen are eternal."*
> **2 Corinthians 4:18**

With these things in mind we can move into the place of growth and enlargement. **Romans 8:37** calls us more than conquerors. That means we receive increase from every conflict and trial as they always provide rewards and spoils. We always come out with more than we started.

The yetzer is the tool we have been given to see what the Father is doing and to join Him! The joy of being spiritually minded is how it strengthens our relationship with one another and with our Father.

Son Glasses - Seeing The Unseen

> *"Then Jesus answered and said to them, "Most assuredly, I say to you, the Son can do nothing of Himself, but what He sees the Father do; for whatever He does, the Son also does in like manner. For the Father loves the Son, and shows Him all things that He Himself does; and he will show Him greater works than these, that you may marvel."* **John 5:19-20**

There is a space in between the spiritual realm and the physical called the unseen realm. This is the place where the substance of what we perceive to be real is stored and energized.

Hebrews 11:3 says the worlds are framed by the Word of God. Matter seems solid to us, but at the quantum level, matter is made of sound.

The physical world is much like a hologram that projects the reality of the unseen realm. The unseen could be considered the source code, the spiritual heavenly realm is the hologram computer, and what we see physically is the projection. The source code is the reality and what we see is only a projection.

Quantum Physics and Quantum Mechanics have taught us that physical is made up of both particles and waves. These are sometimes called wave packets. They are essentially packets of potential. They are collapsed to become their intended purpose.[33]

We participate in this process with the use of our words. We call forth the potential of God's Word (blessing) or the curses of the fallen world. That is why when we believe and speak, it brings our outer world into alignment with the inner reality of the Spirit.

> *"And since we have the same spirit of faith, according to what is written,' I believed and therefore I spoke,' we also believe and therefore speak,"* **2 Corinthians 4:13**

> *"That if you confess with your mouth the Lord Jesus and believe in your heart that God has raised Him from the dead, you will be saved."* **Romans 10:9**

We can understand this when we consider that the spoken Word of God called the world and all we can see into existence.

That is why we call Jesus the Creator. He is the Living Word (LOGOS). The physical world is made up of vibrations or frequencies that we are able to perceive as physical. These frequencies are the voice of God.

> *"While we do not look at the things which are seen, but at the things which are not seen. For the things which are seen are temporary, **but the things which are not seen are eternal.**"*
> **2 Corinthians 4:18**

> *"Now faith is the substance of things hoped for, the evidence of things not seen. For by it the elders obtained a good testimony. **By faith we understand that the worlds were framed by the word of God, so that the things which are seen were not made of things which are visible.**"*
> **Hebrews 11:1-3**

> "God, who at various times and in various ways spoke in time past to the fathers by the prophets, has in these last days spoken to us by **His Son, whom He has appointed heir of all things, through whom also He made the worlds**; who being the brightness of His glory and the express image of His person, and **upholding all things by the word of His power**, when He had by Himself purged our sins, sat down at the right hand of the Majesty on high." **Hebrews 1:1-3**

The yetzer gives us the capacity to draw upon the more real realm of the unseen. We do not use blind hope or guesses, but rather tap into a very real substance of God's raw creative power.

The fact that we can perceive the physical world around us is proof that our yetzer is functioning. We don't actually see the world outside of ourselves, but rather the eyes are sending a signal to the brain. It is in our mind that we process the picture and make an imaginary projection based on our frame of reference. This is the same process that allows us to see the spiritual and unseen realms. That means that what we believe to be "real" is simply an imaginary projection in our mind. It is real, but our perception of it is only a projection in our mind.

The Lord has amazing exploits planned for us that us. We are so often constrained to logical thinking and limitation by submitting to our own thoughts and understanding.

Doesn't that make it easier to consider seeing and living out from the realm of the unseen?

> *"For though by this time you ought to be teachers, you need someone to teach you again the first principles of the oracles of God; and you have come to need milk and not solid food. For everyone who partakes only of milk is unskilled in the word of righteousness, for he is a babe. **But solid food belongs to those who are of full age, that is, those who by reason of use have their senses exercised to discern both good and evil.**"* **Hebrews 5:12-14**

Once we begin to mature and exercise these spiritual senses, the spiritual will become more real to us than the physical. This is the place of sonship that our Father is preparing us to enjoy together.

The new spirit we receive when we believe is a baby. We must help it to grow through use and mature beyond milk drinking to be able to process the meat of the Word.

Repent - Mindshift

"For you know that afterward, when he wanted to inherit the blessing, he was rejected, for he found no place for repentance, though he sought it diligently with tears." **Hebrews 12:17**

*"in humility correcting those who are in opposition, **if God perhaps will grant them repentance**, so that they may know the truth,"* **2 Timothy 2:25**

Repentance not something we do, but rather something God does for us. The key to understanding it is in the origin of the word. It is the translated Greek word μετανοέω (metanoia).[34]

The literal meaning of "metanoia" is "a change of mind." "Meta" means "change" and "Noia" means "mind." Repentance therefore means a supernatural "change of mind."

Repentance is, therefore, the Spirit of God coming within and upon us to supernaturally tune us into the frequency of Heaven. It is a shift from being carnally minded, to spiritually minded in Christ.

The phrase "repent of sin" is not specifically found in the Scriptures. There is a similar phrase in **Acts 20:21**, "repentance toward God," and "faith toward our Lord Jesus Christ." This principle can be seen in **2 Corinthians 3:16** in which the Holy Spirit says that the veil is lifted when we turn to the Lord. It is in looking to Him that we are changed inwardly and our behavior is the result of this shift in thinking.

The repenting for sins concept is really a religious term based on works that are not the result of faith, but on human effort.

We find a similar word used in Scripture 3 times by the Holy Spirit: μεταμορφόω (**Metamorphoo**). This is the word translated as transfiguration and transformation of the mind. Repentance is again, related to the supernatural work of the Holy Spirit to change our thinking to align with the mind of Christ.

This is important because we cannot have faith in Jesus Christ unless we have changed our thinking about Him being Lord. Some have trusted in Him as Savior, but have they really changed their mind about His Lordship?

> *"Therefore I make known to you that no one speaking by the Spirit of God calls Jesus accursed, and no one can say that Jesus is Lord except by the Holy Spirit."* **1 Corinthians 12:3**

Notice in this Scripture that Paul writes to the Corinthians about how godly sorrow produces the change of mind or repentance. Sorrow is not repentance, but can be part of the process of His working in us.

> *"Now I rejoice, not that you were made sorry, but that your sorrow led to repentance. For you were made sorry in a godly manner, that you might suffer loss from us in nothing. For godly sorrow produces repentance leading to salvation, not to be regretted; but the sorrow of the world produces death."* **2 Corinthians 7:9-10**

It is a fact, that the goodness of God can cause us to feel sorrow. This is a relational issue. There is a difference between being sad about suffering consequences and being sorry we hurt someone we care about by our actions.

> *"We love Him because He first loved us."* **1 John 4:19**

> *"Or do you despise the riches of His goodness, forbearance, and longsuffering, not knowing that the goodness of God leads you to repentance?"* **Romans 2:4**

Believing is another way to see repentance. When we move from unbelief to belief, it is a supernatural shift from the natural to the supernatural. Prayerfully examine these examples: (**Acts 2:38; 3:19; 5:31; 8:22; 11:18; 17:30; 20:21; 26:20**).

Conviction Or Guilt?

When the Lord Jesus told the disciples that the Holy Spirit would be sent to convict the world of sin, this has become misunderstood to be His ministry to the believer as well.

> *"And when He has come, He will convict the world of sin, and of righteousness, and of judgment:"* **John 16:8**

This is an important distinction because it is often believed that the Holy Spirit is judging our sin in real-time and convicting us of sin.

In **Acts 1:8** Jesus said that when the Holy Spirit came upon us we would, "receive power to be His witnesses." This is the ministry of the Holy Spirit.

The Spirit has been sent to testify of Christ in us and through us. His is a ministry of glory and life that transforms us. He is not pointing out what is wrong with us, but is rather moving us towards our identity in Christ. He is pulling us closer to the Father at every moment, it is our part to tune into Him and draw upon His life and glory. He is our food.

Much of what people call the conviction of the Holy Spirit is the result of false humility. How is that possible? Guilt is never from God and is the result of walking in the flesh. If we are not spiritually minded, we are in the flesh. There is no neutral ground. It is one side or the other. If He is not leading us, we are in the flesh and at enmity with God.

"For to be carnally minded is death, but to be spiritually minded is life and peace. Because the carnal mind is enmity against God; for it is not subject to the law of God, nor indeed can be. **So then, those who are in the flesh cannot please God."** **Romans 8:6-8**

The Holy Spirit leads us into our destiny in the convergence of all things to Christ. The conviction He is bringing to the world is of the goodness of Christ. When we see Jesus Christ He changes us. We are transformed by beholding Him inwardly and through one another. Can you see Him in others? We are His Body so that is what we should be watching for:

"Therefore, from now on, we regard no one according to the flesh. Even though we have known Christ according to the flesh, yet now we know Him thus no longer. Therefore, if anyone is in Christ, he is a new creation; old things have passed away; behold, all things have become new.

Now all things are of God, who has reconciled us to Himself through Jesus Christ, and has given us the ministry of reconciliation, that is, that God was in Christ reconciling the world to Himself, not imputing their trespasses to them, and has committed to us the word of reconciliation."
2 Corinthians 5:16-19

Our sins were judged and, therefore, forgiven in Jesus Christ at the cross. It is His pleasure to reveal our righteousness in Christ as the gift of all gifts. He is working in us to call out our destiny in Christ among one another.

"There is therefore now no condemnation to those who are in Christ Jesus, who do not walk according to the flesh, but according to the Spirit. For the law of the Spirit of life in Christ Jesus has made me free from the law of sin and death. For what the law could not do in that it was weak through the flesh, God did by sending His own Son in the likeness of sinful flesh, on account of sin: He condemned sin in the flesh that the righteous requirement of the law might be fulfilled in us

who do not walk according to the flesh but according to the Spirit. For those who live according to the flesh set their minds on the things of the flesh, but those who live according to the Spirit, the things of the Spirit. For to be carnally minded is death, but to be spiritually minded is life and peace. Because the carnal mind is enmity against God; for it is not subject to the law of God, nor indeed can be. So then, those who are in the flesh cannot please God." **Romans 8:1-8**

Repentance Births Supernatural Knowledge

"....we have not stopped praying for you and asking God to fill you with the knowledge of his will through all spiritual wisdom and understanding." **Colossians 1:9**

The process begins with knowledge and then moves us toward spiritual wisdom and understanding. The Greek word Paul used for knowledge is epignōsis (eh-PIG-noh-sis).[35] The context of epignosis is that the Word of God possesses us and we become the very will of God in experience. It is a full experiential knowledge of the heart that defines our reality. This word was used twenty times in the New Testament letters.

Epignosis is much more than head knowledge and becomes our frame of reference in which we view and respond to reality. It is a complete shifting in our spiritual mind that overrides our natural thinking. It occurs when the Word "knows" us. The "knowing" becomes the lens that we view reality through. We come into a pure harmony with the truth and can see everything as it really is and not only as things appear to our natural senses. This Spirit induced paradigm shift transcends "Son glasses" as we begin to have our Father's eyes and see events and people through His perspective of love and goodness.

Priests & Kings

We are called to have abundance for every good work. This is a flow through promise. Here is how it works: As we are giving, God will replenish and multiply the resources to meet the needs of others to the praise of His glory.

The Dead Sea is dead because it a low point and living streams that pour into it become dead as they mix with the dead water. There is no outflow.

The point is that God does not intend to pool resources with us. If we do that, we dry and or become poisoned. The Kingdom blessings are given to us as resources to serve the world as priests and kings.

It is not easy to be a cheerful giver when you are digging ditches and scratching dusty coins out of your pocket. On the other hand, when the provision is replenishing as fast as you can give it and multiplying at the same time, that is fun and hilarious. That is how you become a **2 Corinthians 9:7** cheerful giver.

The resources of God are supplied to us through the glory. All our needs to accomplish the task of God have already been placed into us. We simply need to release by faith what God has already given us. The glory of God is in the Ekklesia.

> *"And my God shall supply all your need according to His riches in glory by Christ Jesus."* **Philippians 4:19**

If we call the power company every time we want to cook popcorn, they are going to think we are crazy. They will simply tell us we are already a power customer and to turn on the microwave.

"Now to Him who is able to do exceedingly abundantly above all that we ask or think, according to the power that works in us, to Him be glory in the church by Christ Jesus to all generations, forever and ever. Amen" **Ephesians 3:20-22**

*"But this I say: He who sows sparingly will also reap sparingly, and he who sows bountifully will also reap bountifully. So let each one give as he purposes in his heart, not grudgingly or of necessity; for God loves a cheerful giver. **And God is able to make all grace abound toward you, that you, always having all sufficiency in all things, may have an abundance for every good work.**"* **2 Corinthians 9:6-9**

There is a prevailing misunderstanding in the world about our role on this planet. We are born from the Spirit of Heaven and are such now Kingdom citizens placed here to be trained to rule and to reign with Christ for eternity.

While some may grasp this future aspect of our role as kings, we must also understand that we are to take our place today as a royal priesthood and bring to earth the very authority of the Kingdom of God. Peter calls us a royal priesthood. This speaks to the priesthood of all believers. Religious tyrants have gone astray throughout history and created a hierarchical elite priesthood while craftily hiding this birthright from the Body of Christ.

We are not saved and waiting to go to Heaven as commonly believed. Salvation through the cross is much more. The cross is not an end in itself, but is rather a doorway to an incredible new life in Christ. We are given the keys to all things and are called to reign in this life as servant kings.[36]

"For if by the one man's offense death reigned through the one, much more those who receive abundance of grace and of the gift of righteousness will reign in life through the One, Jesus Christ." **Romans 5:17**

The Order of Melchizedek

"For this Melchizedek, king of Salem, priest of the Most High God, who met Abraham returning from the slaughter of the kings and blessed him, to whom also Abraham gave a tenth part of all, first being translated "king of righteousness," and then also king of Salem, meaning "king of peace," without father, without mother, without genealogy, having neither beginning of days nor end of life, but made like the Son of God, remains a priest continually." **Hebrews 7:1**

One could say *Melchizedek* was a type and shadow of Christ, or more probable a pre-incarnate visit of the Word Himself. Scripture seems to support the latter version because He brought bread and wine to the meeting. What we know for certain is:

"For it is evident that our Lord arose from Judah, of which tribe Moses spoke nothing concerning priesthood. And it is yet far more evident if, in the likeness of Melchizedek, there arises another priest who has come, not according to the law of a fleshly commandment, but according to the power of an endless life. For He testifies: 'You are a priest forever According to the order of Melchizedek.'" **Hebrews 7:14-17**

There is a dynamic to the royal priesthood that is very exciting. There have been 3 official royal priests: **Melchizedek**, **Jesus**, and the **Body of Christ**.

King David – A Royal Priest Prototype

King David was a prototype of the royal priesthood as he was a king who transcended the Levitical priesthood. It was his revelation of the higher order that allowed him to wear an ephod, eat showbread and bring new covenant worship to the Tabernacle of David.[37]

What is the order?

"For He testifies: 'You are a priest forever According to the order of Melchizedek'" **Hebrews 7:17**

The royal priesthood actually follows a principle called an order. It could be considered the will of God being channeled through men through an eternal priesthood. The word order is very powerful and has its origin in the Hebrew word for generation. The original text uses the Hebrew word DOR (The origin of the English word Order), which was used in context of a man entering and leaving a tent. It also represents going full circle. When combined these mean "the movement of man," a generation is the movement through the circle of one man while the next generation is the movement of man through the following circle.

The ancient Hebrew saw time as a circle. **Genesis 1:1** says, "in a beginning" (bereshiyt means in "a" beginning, not "the" beginning).

This world was cursed at the fall of Adam. The world begins anew with the new order of things and is destroyed again at the flood. The world begins anew and will be destroyed again and recreated at the end as the new creation is manifested.[38]

The act of creation was God's power releasing His will through the Word to call the chaos into order. When God placed man in dominion over the earth, He was channeling His authority through man.

When we align with the prophetic testimony of Jesus Christ we are in a mutual priesthood and become partakers of His power and authority. God now expresses and distributes His kingdom through the royal priesthood. This is not a religious principle, but is rather God's relational government in action.

King of Kings

"And He has on His robe and on His thigh a name written: KING OF KINGS AND LORD OF LORDS." **Revelation 19:16**

Lord Jesus is King of His Kingdom and we also are called kings. We carry a kingly anointing that has substantial benefits in this world that assist us in performing the other aspect of our assignment as priests of reconciliation.

When a king conquered a territory in ancient times, he took responsibility for the citizens of the conquered territory. The kingly anointing we have received is not for our personal gain and rule, but rather affords us royal access to the throne of God, an inheritance, and the family name.

It is the proper use of these elements that enables us to draw upon heavenly resources to impact the world around us and serve others in demonstrations of provision, spiritual power, and love.

The blessings of God are not ours to pool up, but are rather released through us in a flow-through dynamic. This is the nature of the supernatural life of God in us. The fullness we experience is the result of overflow. There is never lack in overflow.

There is no end to the increase of God's Kingdom!

"Of the increase of His government and peace there will be no end, upon the throne of David and over His kingdom." **Isaiah 9:7**

Our kingly anointing impacts every element of society and especially in business and the marketplace. The Levitical Priests were not allowed to own property. Royal priests work from both dynamics of being a king who is reigning in this life and as a priest reconciling the world to God through the ministry of glory.

Every passing day brings us into increase. As we convert our physical activities into spiritual assets, we grow and increase spiritually every day and are transformed glory by glory by the Spirit of the Lord.

The 99% principle is even more exciting with the royal priesthood in view. We have an anointing in Christ to expand the Kingdom of God in all areas of our life. We spend the majority of our week in the marketplace rather than the meeting place (Church Meetings).

Again we can unite on the 99% and there is so much need and ministry opportunity that there are opportunities for everyone to love, encourage, bless and minister the gifts of the Holy Spirit as Kings and Priests.

When we see the marketplace as a place of ministry rather than a job or business, we can also conduct spiritual warfare as we usurp the trespassing spiritual forces in our respective work assignments. We rule over the forces of darkness and serve the people. That is our royal duty.

Whoever controls the spiritual atmosphere of any location has the victory in the physical realm as well. The entire purpose is the relationships. Everything that the Lord is doing in the world today is relational.

The Holy Spirit has been sent to work together with us to conform the children of God into the image of our Brother, Jesus Christ. Any increase is geared towards this end in mind.

The measure of the Kingdom of God is proportional to the

measure of Christ manifest among His Body. The Kingdom and the glory are directly tied to Him and they are the direct result of His Presence.

The royal priesthood is also sometimes individualized. There is no specific Scripture that calls us a priest, but rather we are called in **1 Peter 2:9,** "a royal priesthood and a holy nation."

> *"For there is one God and one Mediator between God and men, the Man Christ Jesus.*" **1 Timothy 2:5**

The priesthood is not expressed when we try to act as an independent mediator, but rather when we bring the Mediator Himself into a matter as we embody Him. We are His Body and He is the High Priest. The power of the Ekklesia is always in gathering in His name:

> *"For where two or three are gathered together in My name, I am there in the midst of them."* **Matthew 18:20**

Chapter Three
Christ Is Community

"For as the body is one and has many members, but all the members of that one body, being many, are one body, so also is Christ. For by one Spirit we were all baptized into one body—whether Jews or Greeks, whether slaves or free—and have all been made to drink into one Spirit. For in fact the body is not one member but many." **1 Corinthians 12:12-14**

"Then those who gladly received his word were baptized; and that day about three thousand souls were added to them. And they continued steadfastly in the apostles' doctrine and fellowship, in the breaking of bread, and in prayers. Then fear came upon every soul, and many wonders and signs were done through the apostles. Now all who believed were together, and had all things in common, and sold their possessions and goods, and divided them among all, as anyone had need. So continuing daily with one accord in the temple, and breaking bread from house to, they ate their food with gladness and simplicity of heart, praising God and having favor with all the people. And the Lord added to the church daily those who were being saved." **Acts 2:41-47**

"Do you not know that you are the temple of God and that the Spirit of God dwells in you? If anyone defiles the temple of God, God will destroy him. For the temple of God is holy, which temple you are." **1 Corinthians 3:16-17**

Eternal Koinonia

Community is an eternal principle that is found in the relationship of the Godhead. The Father, Son and Holy Spirit have been in fellowship together for eternity.

Before there was a creation, there was the Godhead. God is an eternal community of life, love and fellowship. The most powerful form of communication is ZOE. Life is eternally shared or communicated among the Godhead.

This life sharing fellowship consists of three Persons; the Father, the Son and the Holy Spirit. The New Testament refers to this community as the Godhead.

In the Hebrew language, they are called Elohiym. They are the same Ones Who said, "Let Us make man in Our image and likeness."[39] The word "fellowship" comes from the Greek word: koinwniða – (koinonia) which literally means: communion, sharing in common, communication and partnership. The three members of the Godhead continually communicate their life and love with another.[40]

The word koinonia is not exclusive to the Godhead as it is used repeatedly throughout the New Testament. It is usually translated as fellowship. Our fellowship is a sharing of life and love through a communion with one another in the power of the Holy Spirit. We are called through the gospel to enter into this same koinonia or fellowship together with the Father, in Christ and through the Holy Spirit.

The convergence principle in Christ is God's will working throughout the universe to sum up all things in Christ as the firstborn among many brethren.

Convergence – Summing Up All Things In Christ

The Godhead consists of the Father, Son and Holy Spirit.[41]
We are called into the same oneness with the Father that Jesus
had throughout eternity. **Romans 8:17** tells us that we are co-
heirs with Christ. We who are in Christ are now in eternal
fellowship with the Godhead. That's a mind blower!

We are the Body of Christ and the fullness of the Godhead
dwells in His Body. We are in Christ and Christ is in us.[42] We
are members of His Body and therefore members of the
Godhead. The Father is obviously running things, but allows us
to have a say in matters. That is the privilege of prayer.

When Satan was tempting Jesus in the wilderness, the focus of
the temptation was His identity as the Son of God.[43] The
temptation was to perform something to prove His identity. His
responses demonstrated that we are to live in our identity by
faith and not by performance.

Our identity is Christ. He is our life, our source, and the
substance of the glory. Christ in us is the hope of glory.[44] It is no
longer we who live, but Christ that lives in us.[45]

Our oneness with the Godhead is such that we can now make
the following statement:

> *Jesus said to him, "Have I been with you so long, and yet you
> have not known Me, Philip? He who has seen Me has seen
> the Father; so how can you say, 'Show us the Father'?"*
> **John 14:9**

The amazing Covenant made with us demonstrates God's
generosity and overwhelming grace. We got the better end of
the deal. He has pooled our resources together, so to speak.

What is ours is now His and what is His is now ours. That is
how a marriage works. We are united as one in Christ. We are
now participants in the eternal koinonia of the Godhead.

> *"For we are members of His body, of His flesh and of His bones. "For this reason a man shall leave his father and mother and be joined to his wife, and the two shall become one flesh." This is a great mystery, but I speak concerning Christ and the church."* **Ephesians 5:3-32**

Lord Jesus has this same perspective towards us. When Paul the apostle was an unbeliever (Saul), it was his mission to destroy the followers of Jesus. When Lord Jesus appeared to him on the Road to Damascus, He essentially told Saul that what he was doing to the disciples he was doing to Him.

> *"Then Saul, still breathing threats and murder against the disciples of the Lord, went to the high priest and asked letters from him to the synagogues of Damascus, so that if he found any who were of the Way, whether men or women, he might bring them bound to Jerusalem.*
>
> *As he journeyed he came near Damascus, and suddenly a light shone around him from heaven. Then he fell to the ground, and heard a voice saying to him, 'Saul, Saul, why are you persecuting Me?' And he said, 'Who are You, Lord?' Then the Lord said, 'I am Jesus, whom you are persecuting.'"* **Acts 9:1-5**

1 Corinthians 3:16 uses the plural Greek word for "you" (*este*), "you are the Temple of God" because we are collectively the Body of Christ and His Body is the Temple. One of the accusations against Jesus was His claim that He threatened to destroy the Temple. They did not understand that He was talking about His own Body.

> *"This fellow said, 'I am able to destroy the Temple of God and to build it in three days."* **Matthew 26:61**

God is building us together as living stones to make up one building in Christ and not independent or mini Temples. Saying, "I am the Temple" individualizes this vital corporate reality.

Christ In The Center

When the Holy Spirit is gathering people together, there is a destiny and purpose in the relationships. The people the Lord is orchestrating into our life are part of our inheritance and our assignment. This includes jobs, neighbors, friends and family.

We look to Him to live out His life in and among us. The mission is a family flowing together in a Spirit empowered purpose.

Relationship is the important dynamic to all true Spirit led life and ministry. Seeing the center of all things summed up in Christ facilitates our relationships. Any type of organization must be relational and people can be deployed based on Spiritual function and not just necessity.

That means we are not filling static positions, but are rather remaining mobile and adaptive to the flow of the Spirit. Rather than a program or a system, we use values as frameworks.

The core value is linked to the Person of Jesus Christ and the core of His teaching to love God with our whole heart, to love others even as we are loved By God and to have a lifestyle of intentional disciple making.[46]

We need not look for things to do to be missional, but rather ask the main Missionary Himself what His plan is and how He wills to use us. Our schedule becomes prophetic and apostolic as the Holy Spirit guides us into our day. Rather than simply shopping, we go make disciples and pick up a few things while we are out.

The first century believers walked in signs and wonders and the way they lived also caused a sense of awe and wonder. We too can be a sign and a wonder to the world by the way we live. The activities of spirit led missional living are simple.

The overlying element of their life is that they lived in the light and reality that Jesus was among them through the power of the Holy Spirit. They lived an obvious life of celebration.

Acts 2:42–47 The First Century Believers Set Our Example:

They listened to the apostles' teaching.
They "fellowshipped."
They "broke bread."
They prayed.
They "lived" together.
They shared their possessions.
They gave to the needy.
They met daily in the temple courts.
They ate together.

They were not acting missional, doing outreaches, or conducting services, yet at the end of this list, Luke records that, "the Lord added to their number daily those who were being saved."

These activities were the mission. Being the church is about our identity and not something we cultivate in a neutral location. So much of church activity today consists of a few songs, a prayer and a sermon. If this were going to start a revolution, it would have happened by now.

There is a perceived need to have special evangelism programs because many believers have not aligned to a mission-minded lifestyle. We are the Body of Christ. He is embodied in our lives.

Can you imagine going to Africa as a missionary and not engaging your neighbors with the good news? How can we not do so in our current mission field at home?

Community Discipleship

Discipleship is sharing life with one another as members of Christ's Body. It is not about teaching information. Our part is to position one another to experience an inward transformation by the power of the Holy Spirit. It is not an information exchange, but rather about spiritual life. The Law of The Spirit of Life has delivered us from the Law of Sin and Death. We are sharing the life of Christ with one another as He conforms us inwardly to the image of Christ.

The gifts of the Spirit manifest Christ to one another as a fail-safe from independence. There is no "me and Jesus." It takes every part doing its share in order for us to reach our potential. When God speaks to us, we must realize that He is not dealing with us as independent individuals. The Head is rather speaking to the parts of His Body through us to one another.

Individually, we do not have the mind of Christ. **1 Corinthians 2:16** says, "WE have the mind of Christ." That means when we are saying, "I" have the mind of Christ, we are individualizing and missing both the power and blessing of the statement.

True discipleship includes the practice of Spirit led relational communities discipling one another and results in the expansion of the Kingdom.

Spirit led relational communities are the vehicle that the Holy Spirit uses to draw people into the Kingdom. Luke said, "Everyone was filled with awe." This was not so much from the signs and wonders done by the apostles, as it was the love demonstrated by the believers. Jesus said in **John 21** that when we demonstrate oneness, the world would believe He was sent. Our oneness is a sign and a wonder.

Christis Community

Living as interconnected members of Christ in our homes, neighborhoods, and cities is a powerful testimony. This is also the vehicle that God uses to reveal Himself and to transform us into the image of Christ.

Don't make the mistake of idealism when it comes to these communities. Experience and Scriptural records indicate they are messy and the hardest thing we will ever do. The truth is, the results make it worth every moment.

Community can be very challenging but in the end, God is always glorified and we are always transformed by His glory. We make mistakes in relationships, but forgiveness and love always win. Community living and discipleship that demonstrate those fruits attract people to the Kingdom!

The object is for the Kingdom of God to be represented in our communities and work environments with real, living awe-inspiring lighthouses that demonstrate the oneness and love of Jesus Christ living in and among us.

If our focus in on filling seats in a meeting, getting soul winning notches on a belt, building a membership, or finding other outward measurements to point at, we have missed the mark.

Our faith in Jesus Christ is not a religious or organizational lifestyle. We are rather called to be co-heirs with Christ and members of the Royal Household. The life we live together on this planet is a time of preparation to mature into our purpose together in Christ. He is working all things to together in our lives to accomplish this eternal purpose.

Sonship - Inheritance

The Inheritance of All Things

In order for the Body of Christ to fulfill the greater works of the end-time, we must be in a balance of intimacy and authority as members of the Household of God.

> *"Now I plead with you, brethren, by the name of our Lord Jesus Christ, that you all speak the same thing, and that there be no divisions among you, but that you be perfectly joined together in the same mind and in the same judgment. For it has been declared to me concerning you, my brethren, by those of Chloe's household, that there are contentions among you. Now I say this, that each of you says, 'I am of Paul,' or 'I am of Apollos,' or 'I am of Cephas,' or 'I am of Christ.' Is Christ divided? Was Paul crucified for you? Or were you baptized in the name of Paul?"* **1 Corinthians 1:10-13**

It is not acceptable for us to be separated by our flesh. The Holy Spirit will move us further as a corporate expression of Christ and manifest the all things ministry of our inheritance. This is possible when we move into the full expression of the corporate Christ in and among us.

> *"All things that the Father has are Mine. Therefore I said that He will take of Mine and declare it to you."* **John 16:15**

> *"He who did not spare His own Son, but delivered Him up for us all, how shall He not with Him also freely give us all things?"* **Romans 8:32**

The inheritance we have received is on par with our Brother, the Firstborn. He has sent the Comforter to "declare" to us the inheritance of "all things."[47] In order for us to take our place of sonship and draw upon the resources of Heaven, it must be revealed to us supernaturally.

Revelation is the principle of unveiling our minds to see the glory of God and the fullness of our inheritance that is based on the abundance of God.

We must present ourselves to the Father as a living sacrifice so that we can be transformed in our thinking. It is His good pleasure to declare to us our inheritance.

While we may understand this important detail intellectually, we must yield ourselves to the Holy Spirit's ministry of adoption. He wants us to inwardly experience the Father's love and blessing to the degree that mere words cannot express the reality and power of His love.

The only word that would satisfy would be Abba (Daddy) and it should well up in us in as a powerful revelation that is a spontaneous outcry of love and joy.

It is important to distinguish the difference between "children of God" and "sons of God."

This is addressed in **Romans 8:14-21**. The Spirit bears witness with their spirit that they are "children of God," and, as such, they are His heirs and joint-heirs with Christ.

There is a difference between birth into the kingdom and maturity.

> *"...as many as are led by the Spirit of God, these are sons of God."* **Romans 8:14**

This intimacy and obedience demonstrates the character and relationship of maturity. It is time for the Body of Christ to walk in the power of the Spirit of adoption.

Adoption - From Child To Son

"Unto us a child is born, unto us a son is given" **Isaiah 9:6**

τέκνον (Teknon)

- **John 1:12; 11:52**
- **Romans 8:16-17, 21; 9:8**
- **Philippians 2:15**
- **I John 3:1-2, 10**

Teknon is the Greek word used to describe a descendant by birth. It is usually translated as "children," when speaking about believers in Christ. John uses it exclusively this way. Christians are declared to be children of God (**John 1:12; I John 3:1-2,10**), having been born into His family. This word could actually be translated as "a born-one."[48]

υἱός (Huios)

- **Matthew. 5:9**
- **Luke 20:36**
- **Romans 8:14, 19**
- **Galatians 3:26**

Huios is the Greek word used for a legal adoption. Paul's use of the huios is placed within the very context of the Greek word: **υἱοθεσία (Huiothesia) meaning, "the placing of sons,"**[49] **used in Romans. 8:15 and Galatians 4:5-7**. Adoption was an important principle in the ancient Greek world.[50]

Adoption Means: Placing of Sons

We think of adoption in terms of taking a child from one family or a child with no family and making it a member of another. This is very different from the Greek or Roman adoption where the father adopted as a son his own child. Through birth: a child (teknon); Through a public adoption or "placing:" declared a son (huios).[51]

There was a preparation time between the period of birth and adoption called growth, education and discipline. The child was trained until maturity and then brought into public adoption into sonship.

Adoption occurred when the son was publicly recognized as one who could faithfully represent the father. He had arrived at the point of maturity, where the father could entrust him with the responsibility of overseeing the family business. In Roman adoptions, the father would declare in the marketplace something like, "This is my son and I am backing up his word."

Sonship is our position but is also experiential. The son becomes the "heir" of his family's assets and authority. Birth gives us the right to our inheritance, but adoption is how we participate in the inheritance.

> "Then He had been baptized, Jesus came up immediately from the water; and behold, the heavens were opened to Him, and He saw the Spirit of God descending like a dove and alighting upon Him. And suddenly a voice came from heaven, saying, "This is My beloved Son, in whom I am well pleased."
> **Matthew 2:16**

The ultimate end here is that Christ is formed in us to full maturity and there is a chorus of groans waiting on the sons of the kingdom to reach full stature in Christ.[52]

We are on the wrong side of the "until" of Ephesians 4 and all things are moving us in that very direction. Creation is both groaning and waiting for the children to reach maturity and be revealed/adopted as sons.

This adoption is a public declaration of maturity and

assignment of authority. That is our ancient destiny that we were chosen for before the foundation of the world.

Kairos Alignment & Positioning

A significant dynamic of God's provision is eliminating the boundary of time and space. He can position us at the exact time and places necessary to accomplish amazing exploits. When we factor in the blessing power of favor, we are moving in a supernatural flow of resources.

> **Kairos (καιρός)** is an ancient Greek word meaning the right or opportune moment (the supreme moment).

The ancient Greeks had two words for time, chronos and kairos. While the former refers to chronological or sequential time, the latter signifies a time in between, a moment of indeterminate time in which something special happens. What the special something is depends on who is using the word. While chronos is quantitative, kairos has a qualitative nature.[53]

Our Lord is bringing forth a great harvest of souls and within the harvest is every resource necessary to accomplish His will. This requires us to move beyond the chronos index and into the perfect timing of the kairos index.

> *"Therefore lay aside all filthiness and overflow of wickedness, and receive with meekness the implanted word, which is able to save your souls."* **James 1:21**

> *"But Mary kept all these things and pondered them in her heart."* **Luke 2:19**

Like Mary, the biological mother of Jesus, we need to open ourselves to receive what God is saying, even when it is exceedingly abundantly more than we can think or imagine.

While Mary did not understand the things told to her by the angel about the virgin birth, she hid them in her heart.
The Holy Spirit is releasing seeds and planting them in the hearts of those who are humble and they will grow and multiply as our minds are unveiled to the incredible provision and plans for the Lord at this kairos time.

Eternal Now

The past has already gone by and does not exist. The future has not yet happened. When we are in the Spirit, we are living in an eternal NOW. The eternity of the Holy Spirit releases the finished work of the cross and the resurrection power into our lives from inside of us.

We also draw upon the future glorification in the present. We are living out the prophetic testimony of Christ living in us as the hope of glory.

Kairos moments occur as the past, present and future collide in a power packed trio of God's supernatural provision.

The kairos Index is the product of mature sons living and walking in the vision and purpose that is being broadcast and processed by our spirit. We are then being led and directed on the Father's schedule.

Chapter Four

Relational Movement

"For truly against Your holy Servant Jesus, whom You anointed, both Herod and Pontius Pilate, with the Gentiles and the people of Israel, were gathered together to do whatever Your hand and Your purpose determined before to be done.

Now, Lord, look on their threats, and grant to Your servants that with all boldness they may speak Your word, by stretching out Your hand to heal, and that signs and wonders may be done through the name of Your holy Servant Jesus.

And when they had prayed, the place where they were assembled together was shaken; and they were all filled with the Holy Spirit, and they spoke the word of God with boldness."
Acts 4:27-31

Corporate Mission

The Greek word for conveyed is **"rhyomai."**[54] It means to be removed and translated to another location. This can be called a shift.

> *"He has delivered us from the power of darkness and*
> *conveyed us into the kingdom of the Son of His love."*
> **Colossians 1:13**

When we align with the eternal purpose of God and begin to move in the stream of His will, we are shifting to a supernatural atmosphere that fills everything we do and everywhere we go with Christ Himself. That means the atmosphere is anointed with the fragrance of Christ's victory.[55] This makes the ordinary rhythms of our life come alive with supernatural purpose and life.

When we stop seeing ministry as something we add to our schedule we begin to move with gospel intentionality in everything we do. Rather than simply going shopping for groceries, we intentionally go out to make disciples and pick up a few things while we are there.

This offensive intentionality will usurp the forces of darkness in our path. As we walk in fellowship with one another, we walk in the light of God.[56] Light overrides darkness as it dominates any atmosphere. This does not require effort on our part, but is the outflow of our drawing upon the indwelling Spirit of Life. This is the power of the ZOE.

God's will is a converging force in our life moving us towards our destiny. It is the Godhead's eternal purpose to have an image.[57] The purpose of God for our life is to conform us to the image of Christ. This is an image made of many parts and all the parts are equally important. As we live out the Christ life together, He uses every circumstance to move us towards that end.

Multiplication of the Body of Christ occurs supernaturally through each of us as our lives together become an incubator of new birth and supernatural discipleship. That is why we need to shift from an individual mindset into the mind of Christ. We have the mind of Christ as we draw upon Him together.[58]

There is a common evangelism practice in which people are encouraged to receive Christ as their personal Savior. While each of us is held accountable to answer the message of the cross with faith, this is not about a "personal relationship." It is not something that we do alone but rather, the first act is a public baptism to testify of both our death in Christ and our new life as a member of His Body. We are leaving behind the self, and becoming a member of Christ's Body.

Salvation Is Not Personal

The most important shift in living and thinking will be that we are being brought out of our individual lives into a life of purpose and service to God in Christ as a member of His Body.

Colossians 3:4, says, **"Christ Who is our Life."** The key paradigm shift in the New Covenant is that we are called out of our individual lives and into the community of the Body of Christ. We are individual members of a living spiritual organism.

God is a community and our fellowship cannot be one on one. It takes a community to have fellowship with a community. The next section will bring some clarity to this principle.

Homothumadon

A community of believers living the Christ life **(ZOE)** together under the guidance of the Holy Spirit will experience an atmosphere of like-mindedness.

The Greek word used repeatedly ισόμοθυμαδόν-homothumadon.[59] It is a two-part word: homos (same) and thumos (seat of one's soul, passion). It means everyone has a single focused passion: Christ. The closest English words for this principle are to be of "one accord."

The Holy Spirit is revealing the power of community to shift us out of our self-focused lifestyle. Many of us have our own relationship with Jesus, our own faith, our own ministry, our own prayer, our own churches and our own understanding. Christ is our life, not our lives. The Spirit of Life is the Spirit of Christ. Christ is not divided. We are all one in Him. We are drinking from one Spirit.

Whether we all agree, or even feel as though we like one another is inconsequential. We are all drawing upon the same source and He is our life together. This is a universal principle. We as the Body of Christ are connected by birth to one another by the Holy Spirit.

Glocal Vision

Our spiritual connection to other believers in Christ is both local and global. In fact, it is universal as we are plugged into the Body of Christ outside of time and space.

The smallest event in our lives affects every believer worldwide and in Heaven. God may lead us to what seems like a small task to us, but from His view it has cosmic significance. When we obey the Lord's direction in the smallest of matters, it has cosmic repercussions. What seems mundane to us really is part of the convergence principle that God is working all things together to conform us into the image of Christ.

The world population is said to be 7 billion people. That is a staggering amount of people. If only 1 in 3 of the population were believers, that would likely mean there are more believers in the Body of Christ alive than those who have died and are waiting for the Lord's plan to conclude. That means the majority of the Body of Christ is on the planet and positioned to mobilize.

The simple events in our life are part of a greater purpose. **1 Corinthians 12:6** tells us that if one suffers or rejoices we are all impacted through our interconnected life in Christ. Paul understood that even the small matters in His life had cosmic significance in furthering the gospel:

> *"But I want you to know brethren that the things, which happened to me, have actually turned out for the furtherance of the gospel."* **Philippians 1:12**

The Lord Himself creates the single passion. This is not the result of intellectual agreement, but is rather the powerful result of our taking by faith our unity of the Spirit as the Body of Christ. We hold fast the Head of the Body and He infuses us each with like passions to see the will of the Father accomplished.

> *"That they all may be one, even as You, Father, are in Me and I in You, that they also may be in Us; that the world may believe that You have sent Me. And the glory which You have given Me I have given to them, that they may be one, even as We are one..."* ***John 17:21-22***

Community drawing on His Headship produces a Spirit powered oneness. We are one because we are all baptized into one Body. Christ is not separate from His Ekklesia. Where He is, we are and where we are He is also. We are all one in Him. That is the synergistic or holistic power of our being born into a community. This creates a supernatural atmosphere with amazing results.

> *"These all continued with one accord **(homothumadon)** in prayer and supplication, with the women and Mary the mother of Jesus, and with His brothers."* **Acts 1.14**

> *"So continuing daily with one accord **(homothumadon)** in the temple, and breaking bread from house to house, they ate their food with gladness and simplicity of heart."* **Acts 2:46**

> *"And through the hands of the apostles many signs and wonders were done among the people. And they were all with one accord **(homothumadon)** in Solomon's Porch."* **Acts 5:12**

> *" And the multitudes with one accord **(homothumadon)** heeded the things spoken by Philip, hearing and seeing the miracles which he did."* **Acts 8:6**

> *"it seemed good to us, being assembled with one accord **(homothumadon),** to send chosen men to you with our beloved Barnabas and Paul,"* **Acts 15:25**

> *"Now may the God of patience and comfort grant you to be like-minded toward one another, according to Christ Jesus, that you may with one mind **(homothumadon)** and one mouth glorify the God and Father of our Lord Jesus Christ."* **Romans 15:5-6**

Are You Saved?

When declaring the good news of Jesus Christ we can jump-start the apostolic or missional DNA in others by sharing the good news through them. This means we are not trying to get them saved so they can go to Heaven, but rather impart to them God's vision for them to get on track with His eternal purpose of reconciling the world through Christ.

This means rather than asking people if they are "saved and going to Heaven," we should be asking them if they are on track with God's eternal purpose. If we are not living our lives in the light of fellowship and in the power of the Holy Spirit, then we are not even in the game. Some people would answer that they are saved because they have said the sinners' prayer. On the other hand, they probably would not know anything about God's plan for their life or His eternal purpose.

We could even rephrase the question to be something like, "What do you know about the resurrection?" Just be aware that we are pressing a hot button in the spirit realm when we declare the resurrection. This is a sore point for the adversary and he is not pleased when we bring it to light.

The point is that Heaven is not our objective dwelling. God's mind is for Heaven to come to earth. We are not created to be heavenly beings, but more importantly to have new glorified bodies and to live in the physical world manifesting the glory of God. God has become a Man in Jesus Christ so we can live together fellowshipping in His creation.

To understand this fully, it is important to understand that the earth was given to men through Adam. He blew it with his iniquity and brought a curse on the physical world and on us.

The Last Adam, Jesus, has taken all the steps to redeem both fallen man and creation.[60] This is finished but not completely manifest. We are the first fruits or the preview of the new creation. The physical creation according to Romans 8 is groaning with anticipation until the sons of God are fully developed and revealed.

To fully maximize our time on this planet, we must see this life as an extended job interview for the ages to come. Our entrance into the interview is the résumé of Jesus Christ. His résumé is ours. The interview is a formality and the actual job placement program is based on how well we demonstrate our ability to follow instructions in the field. This could also be called on-the-job training.

When we are living our life on mission, we are living out the intentional purpose of God for our life. Our assignment is already planned for us and we must simply present ourselves to God each day. He will bring direct our path to the provision and relationships he is preparing for us.

From The Message Translation:

> *"In your relationships with one another, have the same mindset as Christ Jesus: Who, being in very nature of God, did not consider equality with God something to be used to his own advantage; rather, He made Himself nothing by taking the very nature of a servant being made in human likeness. And being found in appearance as a man, He humbled Himself by becoming obedient to death even death on a cross."* **Philippians 2:5**

Scripture does tell us that when we are absent from the body we go to be present with the Lord.[61] Living eternally floating around Heaven is not God's intention for our future. We may stop in there for a visit, but He has other long-term plans for our lives and for the physical creation.

Convergence – Summing Up All Things In Christ

In Heaven, the martyrs are depicted as though they are looking at their watches and asking about getting the whole thing moving along so they can get back to the planet.

> *"And they cried with a loud voice, saying, "How long, O Lord, holy and true, until You judge and avenge our blood on those who dwell on the earth?"* **Revelation 6:10**

Keep in mind that the future God has planned for us is to have bodies just like Jesus. We are created to be spiritual beings that wear earth suits. We are going to get upgraded earth suit models in the future. The resurrection is our hope, not harps and clouds.

> *"But now Christ is risen from the dead, and has become the first fruits of those who have fallen asleep. For since by man came death, by Man also came the resurrection of the dead. or as in Adam all die, even so in Christ all shall be made alive. But each one in his own order: Christ the first fruits, afterward those who are Christ's at His coming. Then comes the end, when He delivers the kingdom to God the Father, when He puts an end to all rule and all authority and power. For He must reign till He has put all enemies under His feet. The last enemy that will be destroyed is death. For "He has put all things under His feet." But when He says, "all things are put under Him," it is evident that He who put all things under Him is excepted. Now when all things are made subject to Him, then the Son Himself will also be subject to Him who put all things under Him, that God may be all in all.*

> *Otherwise, what will they do who are baptized for the dead, if the dead do not rise at all? Why then are they baptized for the dead? And why do we stand in jeopardy every hour? I affirm, by the boasting in you which I have in Christ Jesus our Lord, I die daily. If, in the manner of men, I have fought with beasts at Ephesus, what advantage is it to me? If the dead do not rise, "Let us eat and drink, for tomorrow we die!"*

Do not be deceived: "Evil company corrupts good habits." Awake to righteousness, and do not sin; for some do not have the knowledge of God. I speak this to your shame.
But someone will say, "How are the dead raised up? And with what body do they come?" Foolish one, what you sow is not made alive unless it dies. And what you sow, you do not sow that body that shall be, but mere grain—perhaps wheat or some other grain. But God gives it a body as He pleases, and to each seed its own body.
All flesh is not the same flesh, but there is one kind of flesh of men, another flesh of animals, another of fish, and another of birds.

There are also celestial bodies and terrestrial bodies; but the glory of the celestial is one, and the glory of the terrestrial is another. There is one glory of the sun, another glory of the moon, and another glory of the stars; for one star differs from another star in glory.

So also is the resurrection of the dead. The body is sown in corruption, it is raised in incorruption. It is sown in dishonor, it is raised in glory. It is sown in weakness, it is raised in power. It is sown a natural body, it is raised a spiritual body. There is a natural body, and there is a spiritual body. And so it is written, "The first man Adam became a living being." The last Adam became a life-giving spirit.

*However, the spiritual is not first, but the natural, and afterward the spiritual. The first man was of the earth, made of dust; the second Man is the Lord from heaven. As was the man of dust, so also are those who are made of dust; and as is the heavenly Man, so also are those who are heavenly. And as we have borne the image of the man of dust, we shall also bear the image of the heavenly Man." **1 Corinthians 15:20-49***

We will be returning to rule and reign with Christ in the millennium and eventually the Heavenly Jerusalem is coming to earth. That is why we are being prepared now to rule and reign with Him as servant kings and priests.

This life is a very short interview for the ages to come. The vital measure is not what we know, but rather what we do for others with what we know. There is a difference between knowing truth and letting the truth define us. When we live in the light of eternity, it empowers us to make decisions that don't benefit our flesh in the short-term, but will bless others for an eternity.

> *"Blessed and holy is he who has part in the first resurrection. Over such the second death has no power, but they shall be priests of God and of Christ, and shall reign with Him a thousand years."* **Revelation 20:6**

> *" Now I saw a new heaven and a new earth, for the first heaven and the first earth had passed away. Also there was no more sea. Then I, John, saw the holy city, New Jerusalem, coming down out of heaven from God, prepared as a bride adorned for her husband. And I heard a loud voice from heaven saying, "Behold, the tabernacle of God is with men, and He will dwell with them, and they shall be His people. God Himself will be with them and be their God."* **Revelation 21:1**

Salvation Is For Today!

Keep in mind that being saved is not a future objective. The moment we entrust ourselves to the Lordship of Jesus Christ, we belong to Him. When we wholly entrust ourselves to Him, we are made whole or "sozo."

> *"We then, as workers together with Him also plead with you not to receive the grace of God in vain. For He says: 'In an acceptable time I have heard you, And in the day of salvation I have helped you.' Behold, now is the accepted time; behold, now is the day of salvation".* **2 Corinthians 6:1-3**

Gospel of Christ
The Good News Is A Person

Salvation is not the starting point of the gospel. Paul received the gospel and it is as follows:

> "Moreover, brethren, I declare to you the gospel which I preached to you, which also you received and in which you stand, by which also you are saved, if you hold fast that word which I preached to you—unless you believed in vain.
>
> For I delivered to you first of all that which I also received: that Christ died for our sins according to the Scriptures, and that He was buried, and that He rose again the third day according to the Scriptures, and that He was seen by Cephas, then by the twelve. After that He was seen by over five hundred brethren at once, of whom the greater part remain to the present, but some have fallen asleep. After that He was seen by James, then by all the apostles. Then last of all He was seen by me also, as by one born out of due time."
> **1 Corinthians 15:1-8**

Unlike the religions of the world, the gospel of Jesus Christ has a verifiable source. Paul said the gospel is according to the Scriptures. The events that transpired in the life of our Lord God in the flesh were detailed in prophecy for several thousand years prior to Him walking them out.

The 4 Amazing Events of The Lord Jesus

Christ Died
Christ Was Buried
Christ Was Raised
Christ Appeared

Convergence – Summing Up All Things In Christ

The gospel is the story of four actual events in the life of Jesus Christ. The good news is a Person. All things are summed up in Him and especially the good news.

> *"Jesus said to him, 'I am the way, the truth, and the life. No one comes to the Father except through Me.'"* **John 14:6**

> *"But of Him you are in Christ Jesus, who became for us wisdom from God—and righteousness and sanctification and redemption"* **1 Corinthians 1:30**

The journey that we begin together is summed up in Christ. The journey is a Person. If we are pursuing truth, then we are pursuing Him. He is the Way, the Truth and the Life. He is also Wisdom, Sanctification and Redemption. These are not doctrines or things we believe, but are rather the result of receiving Him. He brings these with Him.

> *"That if you confess with your mouth the Lord Jesus and believe in your heart that God has raised Him from the dead, you will be saved. For with the heart one believes unto righteousness, and with the mouth confession is made unto salvation."* **Romans 10:9-10**

When we believe In the Lord Jesus, it is not just for salvation. He is not presented in Scripture as a "Personal Savior." When we confess Him as Lord, we are saved. He is Lord first and then saves us from ourselves.

The good news is that Jesus Christ has died for our sins, died for our selves, and has risen again. He has restored the purpose of God and has made possible the new birth. The work is done. We must deliver the message to the world.

He has not come to clean up our lives and make things better. He has rather put into motion a new creation. His plan is very different from self-help programs or even Christian psychology.

We get an entirely new life since the other life is now done away with in the cross.

> *"Therefore, if anyone is in Christ, he is a new creation; old things have passed away; behold, all things have become new"* **2 Corinthians 5:17**

We are the first fruits of the new creation in Christ. A first fruit is a preview of the crop to come. He is the First Fruit and we are in Him.

A first fruit could be viewed like a movie trailer. The movie companies show the best parts of the movie in order to gather interest in people to come and see it in the future.

This is how God is displaying us to the universe. We are God's movie trailer for the new creation. The world and principalities and powers are seeing the manifold wisdom of God in Christ in us and are seeing a foretaste of the new creation.[62]

Jesus Christ is the Good News!

There should be such a celebration and victory in our lives that people ask us to share the good news with them.

As we walk in the fullness of the Holy Spirit, the overflow reaches the needs around us. There is no stealth mode when light is dispelling darkness.

Our testimony is one of bold overcoming power and we need not be ashamed of the good news because it is the power of God unto salvation.[63]

Making Disciples
4 Dimensional Disciple-Making

"Then Jesus came to them and said, 'All authority in heaven and on earth has been given to me. Therefore go and make disciples of all nations, baptizing them in the name of the Father and of the Son and of the Holy Spirit, and teaching them to obey everything I have commanded you. And surely I am with you always, to the very end of the age.'"
Matthew 28:18-20

"And the things that you have heard from me among many witnesses, commit these to faithful men who will be able to teach others also." **2 Timothy 2:2**

Paul demonstrated disciple making to Timothy, who then invested in faithful men, who also passed it on to others.

We are entering a time that many consider to be the end of the ages. There is no longer time to spend years training and waiting for an opportunity to minister to others. Submitting to an authority figure and serving their vision and waiting to function was never God's method of operation. We are born into our life in Christ equipped with everything we will need. When we put off old paradigms and traditions, we position ourselves for the supernatural acceleration of God's work in us.

We are called into a supernatural and exciting daily adventure. The literal translation of the command in **Matthew 28:19-20** is this: **"As you are going, make disciples!"** Jesus is directing us to make disciples as we go about doing life.

When we truly become a supernatural disciple of the Lord Jesus, we enter into a lifelong process and are essentially becoming an on-the-job apprentice of Jesus. There is a tangible measurement of this process is in the footprints we leave in the hearts of others each day as we walk with Him.

Lifetime Commitment

Disciple making means bringing new believers into long-term commitments rather than a one-time decision for Christ. They enter into a movement that takes them into a present reality of glory that continues into eternity.

The key to understanding on-the-job training is that we learn by doing, rather than by being simply talked at or sitting and watching others. As Christ begins reaching others through us, we are accelerated in our own transformation.

The word in Greek for disciples is **mathētēs**.[64] The verb that is used means that a believer is a learner or more clearly a learning believer. In other words, we are to make "learning believers" of all nations. It is not simply someone who believes or who learns, but *mathētēs is both elements working in synergy.*

A believing learner is one who places their faith in Christ and makes a lifetime commitment to learn. The Lord said that a disciple is perpetually learning: **John 8:31**, " the one who continues in My Word is the mathetes alethos," or the genuine disciple.

Apprentice Believers

Imagine starting a new painting business and training a new crew how to paint teaching them in an hour weekly class. And if the class is on a Sunday morning when they are not fully awake, how much are they really learning? How long will the training take and will they really know how to paint or train other painters? What if we took them to the job-site and showed them how to paint? They could watch us, then we could do it together, and finally they can paint on their own.

The paint crew would learn quickly and within a few weeks, the painting business could multiply as the crews were training more crews and multiplying the business.

Discipleship is, therefore, not a matter of receiving information, but in believing what God says and obeying. The Hebrew model of disciple making focused more on this type of apprenticeship as the way to transfer knowledge.

Real-Time Discipleship

Practice, correction, and mentoring were applied daily in the first century. This was "just in time" learning that did not ask the learner to memorize information for "just in case" use, but rather new concepts were taught in the moment of application and practice. Accountability was built into the process as the teacher and student lived life together in their daily rhythms and activities.

This will require us to actually invite people into our lives to see the Kingdom in action. When we are living a life in the convergent power of Christ, one day with our family can be a life-changing event for anyone that spends time with us. That is the Christ present reality that He promises us and delivers upon as we rely on Him.

> *"There is only one Life-Leader for you and them-Christ."*
> **Matthew 23:11**

> *"But the anointing which you have received from Him abides in you, and you do not need that anyone teach you; but as the same anointing teaches you concerning all things, and is true,*

and is not a lie, and just as it has taught you, you will abide in Him." **1 John 2:27**

The first step to empowerment is to become a direct follower of the Lord and to see Him as our Teacher. While we have fellow believers and fivefold ministers to assist us, we must begin learning right away to hear His voice and to seek His leadership in all things. That requires a move away from traditional discipleship models that promote dependency on leaders.

First Hand Faith

We have all received a measure of faith. That means we have our own or firsthand faith and need not depend on the faith of others. This empowers us with unshakable conviction.

The power of our fellowship is the "one another" dynamic.

We live our Christ life with interdependence upon one another. It is through the power of community that we are held accountable and encouraged. **When we mutually combine our firsthand faith, we bring powerful spiritual synergy into manifestation.**

Fellowship and community are keys to rapid transformation and fruitfulness. For this reason, we can see how a minimum of three people involved in discipling is very powerful. A one on one dynamic often leads to dependency on the disciple maker. Three people create an instant community that facilitates peer pressure and accountability.

In order to multiply disciples we must be able to affect a single life. Our ministry must impact at least one individual in such a way that they are able duplicate this process again with the next person. This is how a virus is spread — one person at a time as each person carries the contagion.

Discipleship cannot be accomplished from a podium, a video, a book, or any other impersonal technique. We are disciples of Jesus, and He disciples us through one another.

Intentional Focus Values

Jesus was intentional with His schedule and the Spirit arranged every situation as a platform for discipleship. He had a considerable public ministry, but His real heart-transforming ministry was not conducted in this way. The life lessons usually happened in real-time, often while walking, eating, informal gatherings, and sometimes through harsh rebukes.

The key to intentional discipleship is to have a framework or container. The framework is a value system. This makes it possible to also have a visible measurement based on spiritual growth. This means we need to adjust our idea of measuring spiritual success away from counting numbers of seats filled or the amount of money collected. We instead begin looking for inner transformation and fruitfulness through the multiplication of new disciples. These values foster such an environment.

Value System Measurements

- **Is Christ at the center?**
- **Is our community relational?**
- **Do people feel comfortable to participate?**
- **Are people growing in maturity?**
- **Is everyone encouraged to minister?**
- **Is there a visible multiplication?**
- **Is there accountability to truth?**

Just as in the early church, we have access to a process of

Kingdom Building power. This same process is working in places like China today. In the face of terrible opposition and persecution, the growth of the Body of Christ in the "underground church" in China is both explosive and fruitful. A virus is exponentially spread when people are making contact with and infecting others. The virus is the love of God. It is not just a principle or set of values, but is rather a tangible and intoxicating reality brought upon us by the presence of God.

Mobilizing The Laborers

One of the greatest challenges we have is that the harvest is so vast and the laborers few. This may be due to the ministry being presented as some sort of work we "must do." However, Jesus said:

> *"The harvest is plentiful, but the laborers are few; therefore beseech the Lord of the harvest to send out laborers into His harvest."* **Luke 10:2**

There is no lack in the harvest and all the resources including finances and personnel are plentiful. **The laborers are numerous because the lost are also the potential laborers.** The laborers are simply dormant until activated by the gospel.

Laborers may also be already working and working very hard, but not on the right assignment. They may well be serving all sorts of programs and attending many "leadership" meetings, but they are not engaged in the core mission, which is simply making disciples.

As the Holy Spirit orchestrates our daily encounters and relationships, we are positioned into the specific relational assignments He has predestined for us to walk out.

Ministry is relational and any activity that is not producing life and imparting it to others is not really ministry at all. Likewise, many leaders are often so focused on administrative duties; they are not on this assignment either. This comes disguised as an identity crisis. If a person's identity is tied to be a "leader" rather than a "servant" to people, then they have to have many meetings and create opportunities to express themselves as a "leader."

Many leaders are not aware that the mandate to personally make disciples applies to them. Yet, the mission of making disciples was central to the community of the first century believers. Other leaders go the other extreme and exclude the Body from the privilege of disciple making.

Discipling The Nations

The Lord Jesus has broken down the walls and given us the resources to accomplish the great commission. While we are called to disciple nations, we must keep in mind that He will use existing social networks to further this process.

Discipleship must be modeled and effective to be carried to the next generation. It must be a lifestyle.

Our key go-to resource for discipleship training, however, is the Scriptures. Read them out loud with other believers often while expecting Christ to reveal Himself.

Baptized Into Christ

Baptism is a commonly overlooked dynamic to making disciples who make disciples:

> *"Then Jesus came to them and said, 'All authority in heaven and on earth has been given to me. **Therefore go and make disciples of all nations, baptizing them** in the name of the Father and of the Son and of the Holy Spirit, and teaching them to obey everything I have commanded you. And surely I am with you always, to the very end of the age.'"*
> **Matthew 28:18-20**

According to the specific directive of the Lord Jesus, baptizing new disciples is an important component of the disciple making process.

One of the things that limit the multiplication power of disciple making is the belief that only an ordained pastor or minister can baptize a new believer. Some take it further and believe that it requires such professionals just to get someone saved. Can you imagine what would have happened to the Eunuch in Acts 8 if Phillip had told him he could not get baptized until they went into town and found a professional minister or pastor?

> *"I appeal to you, dear brothers and sisters, by the authority of our Lord Jesus Christ, to live in harmony with each other. Let there be no divisions in the church.... I thank God that I did not baptize any of you except Crispus and Gaius, for now no one can say they were baptized in my name. (Oh yes, I also baptized the household of Setphanas baptizing anyone else.) For Christ didn't send me to baptize, but to preach the Good News—and not with clever speech, for fear that the cross of Christ would lose its power."* **1 Corinthians 1:10-17**

While the importance of baptism is significant, the importance of who actually baptizes is less so. Keep in mind that we are not commanded to be baptized. The responsibility is on the disciple maker to baptize the new believer. How can we say we are making disciples if we ignore the first component given us by the Lord Himself? We are to show them the way to obey the message of the cross with the prophetic testimony of baptism.

Baptism - A Prophetic Testimony

> "The Spirit of prophecy is the testimony of Jesus Christ."
> **Revelation 19:1**

Baptism demonstrates two powerful testimonies. The first is that we testify that we are saying good-bye to the old man and reckon him as dead. We are identifying with Christ not only dying for our sins, but also having died, "as us." The second part is in recognizing that He also rose again as the firstborn among many brethren. He becomes both the example of our new life and the source.

Circumcision of The Heart

There is a powerful spiritual dynamic that occurs in the prophetic obedience of baptism. The new covenant purchased with Christ's blood includes a circumcision not made with hands, but by the Spirit in our heart.

> *"In Him you were also circumcised with the circumcision made without hands,* by putting off the body of the sins of the flesh, by the circumcision of Christ, buried with Him in baptism, in which you also were raised with Him through faith in the working of God, who raised Him from the dead"
> **Colossians 2:11-12**

Delivered From Self-Focus

We are plugged in supernaturally as a member of the GLOCAL (local and global) organic Body of Christ. God is a community. We are called to enjoy the Godhead and the community of Christ's Body. The Godhead said in the beginning, "Let us make man in Our image and likeness." The most significant part of our salvation is that it is not personal. We are being birthed by and into the community of the Godhead as we are placed into Christ.

The message of the cross is demonstrated in the prophetic testimony of baptism:

> *"I have been crucified with Christ; it is no longer I who live, but Christ lives in me; and the life, which I now live in the flesh I live by faith in the Son of God, who loved me and gave Himself for me."* **Galatians 2:20**

We are baptized into ONE BODY, not many little self-focused identities and groups. We are delivered from our individualism by our baptism into the community of Christ.

> *"For by one Spirit we were all baptized into one body— whether Jews or Greeks, whether slaves or free—and have all been made to drink into one Spirit."* **1 Corinthians 12:1**

Remember, the word for saved is sozo. It means made whole. We will not be whole until we die to our self and see our life as a member of Christ's Body.

> *"Most assuredly, I say to you, unless a grain of wheat falls into the ground and dies, it remains alone; but if it dies, it produces much grain."* **John 12:24**

While redemption is by grace through faith, there is also a rich spiritual reality that we draw upon in being baptized. We must, in our own act of obedience, ensure we are bringing new believers into the full measure of the disciple making process.

If a person hears the gospel of Jesus Christ and believes in Him as Lord, it makes no sense that they would tell us not to baptize them. We are to teach a new disciple to obey the obvious simple instruction of the Lord. This actually brings the new believer into an encounter with lordship.

They are not getting baptized, but are rather submitting to be baptized. This is also the first act of submitting one to another.

If they tell us they do not want to be baptized, it might be worthwhile to review with them that Jesus is Lord and He has instructed us to baptize new disciples. If they still don't want to be baptized, then leave it at that. We share the truth and God and the new believer are responsible for the results.

Oikos and Baptism

The rich accounts of household evangelism in the Book of Acts demonstrate the powerful testimony of immediate baptism in the presence of the new believers extended family and social networks. This is part of the Lord's powerful plan for multiplication through existing social networks.

When we immediately baptize a new believer in the presence of their extended households and family, it fulfills the first two principles that the Lord instructed us to do in making disciples. That is to baptize and teach them to obey.

Spaces and Places

Strategic use of spaces and places positions us to maximize the spiritual dynamics of our time. In the first century, homes and the marketplace were the primary meeting places for community. In the West, the local church became a common place to establish a community of faith. That dynamic is not the same in today's world.

Strategic Third Places

Six out of ten people may never show an interest in the current model of church services. We must open ourselves to see the Holy Spirit reach the indigenous population in their context. This expands our opportunities to join the Holy Spirit wherever He is working.

The Lord had to appear to Peter in a vision in Luke's account found in **Acts 10:13**. He needed intervention from the Lord to see beyond His current cultural context. His yetzer popped on and God put a vision of the unclean animals upon Peter's imagination as a vision. It took the Lord 3 tries to expand Peter's imagination. We need The Holy Spirit to help us to see beyond our own contexts and to operate with a new level of creative purpose and vision for others.

Worship meetings should be both prophetic and creative. There is no limit to what God can do other than what we impose by our own paradigms and traditions.

The truth is that Jesus Christ is bigger than a meeting and we will bring Him into the context of others as we practice the "as you go" model of discipleship. Some people are not aware that Jesus has any other context than two songs, a prayer, and sermon. This could be the result of drive-by evangelism that is consummated with an invitation to now start "going to our church." There needs to be a contextual delivery of the message. The message of the gospel must be the same, but the context can be fluid.

> Paul said, "...I have become all things to all *men, that I might by all means save some.*" **1 Corinthians 9:22**

People have three main places that they live out their lives. Home, work, and a third place: socializing.

Ray Oldenberg developed the idea of "third places" in his book The Great Good Place. Third places are places or environments where people in the community interact with one another outside the first and second places. The first place is that of the home, and the second place is that of a person's workplace. Oldenburg remarks that "third places" are,

> *"anchors" of community life and facilitate and foster broader, more creative interaction. All societies already have informal meeting places; what is new in modern times is the intentionality of seeking them out as vital to current societal needs... These hallmarks of a true "third place": free or inexpensive; food and drink, while not essential, are important; highly accessible: proximate for many (walking distance); involve regulars – those who habitually congregate there; welcoming and comfortable; both new friends and old should be found there.*[65]

Popular "third places" include coffee shops (such as Starbucks), malls, city parks, exercise facilities, restaurants/pubs and venues for the arts/entertainment.

Some mega churches have tried to emulate popular third

places like coffee shops and restaurants. This seems to make sense. This is really just a more creative way to attract people out of their existing contexts to a neutral zone away from their existing social networks. Remember, our objective is to join the Holy Spirit in His mission to reach the world to reconcile all men to Christ through the gospel.

The Internet and the development of new technologies to communicate by video have created a very predominant electronic third place. This is also a very strategic "location" to watch for direction from the Holy Spirit.

8 Characteristics of Third Places

1. Placed on neutral ground
2. Act as a leveler
3. Conversation is the main activity
4. Allow for accessibility and accommodation
5. Host a stream of regulars
6. Keep a low profile
7. Maintain a playful mood
8. Act as a home away from home

Spaces – The Science of Proximity

There are important social dynamics involved in proximity. People are affected at different depths through proximity. This means that some people do better in intimate environments and others need the anonymity of large social gatherings. Anonymous public spaces are commonly used in modern "church services" and lack long-term heart changing power.

There are four areas of personal territory; public, social, personal, and intimate, that we westerners intuitively respect and use.

Four Dynamic of Spaces

Public space ranges from 12 to 25 feet and is the distance maintained between the audience and a speaker such as the President.

Social space ranges from 4 to 10 feet and is used for communication among business associates, as well as to separate strangers using public areas such as beaches and bus stops.

Personal space ranges from 2 to 4 feet and is used among friends and family members, and to separate people waiting in lines at teller machines, for example.

Intimate space ranges out to one foot and involves a high probability of touching. We reserve it for whispering and embracing.[66]

Real-time disciple making requires us to be sensitive to space and place as we follow the Holy Spirit's plan. By remaining flexible, we are equipped to operate within the context of any culture to facilitate bringing the Kingdom of God.

Jesus often used meals to create an instant intimate space for dealing with matters of the heart. We can also use this amazing strategy as the Holy Spirit sets up dining appointments for His use.

As Paul told the Ephesians, "God can do exceedingly, abundantly more than we can think or imagine."

Ask the Holy Spirit to enlarge your vision like He did with Peter to open new doors of possibility in bringing the Kingdom of God into social contexts that have not been explored.

Table Fellowship
Being A Friend To Sinners

The importance of the meal and whom we share it with must be appreciated in order for us to move into the fullness of multiplying the Body of Christ and moving into God's eternal purpose.

> *"Now when Peter had come to Antioch, I withstood him to his face, because he was to be blamed; for before certain men came from James, he would eat with the Gentiles; but when they came, he withdrew and separated himself, fearing those who were of the circumcision. And the rest of the Jews also played the hypocrite with him, so that even Barnabas was carried away with their hypocrisy.*
>
> *But when I saw that they were not straightforward about the truth of the gospel, I said to Peter before them all, 'If you, being a Jew, live in the manner of Gentiles and not as the Jews, why do you compel Gentiles to live as Jews?'"*
> **Galatians 2:11-14**

The controversy in Antioch was very serious. It was centered on "Table Fellowship." This was again, the purpose of the **Acts 10 vision** revealed to Peter to shift his social paradigms.

This was not simply Jews and Gentiles "eating together." Table fellowship in Judaism was much more than food. This dealt with deeply ingrained social dynamics originating from Jewish purity laws.

The importance of table fellowship is generally underestimated. In the first century church, sharing a table with another person was making a social statement about yourself and about your guest.

Table Fellowship in Judaism was a complex and important issue, especially to the Pharisees. 341 rulings go back to the Pharisees, and 229 are related to table fellowship.[67] The Pharisees were the original elite "Diners Club."

> **"When a simple meal is opened to others, it becomes a subversive, prophetic, and powerful platform of ministry."**

The principle of separation from the unclean is found often in the Gospels. Jesus' friendship and ministry to the "unclean" of their society often confused the Pharisees. He often shared meals with Tax collectors and other "sinners."

Lord Jesus understood that sharing a meal with someone created an instant intimate setting to address important spiritual and heart matters. He demonstrated to us how to erase illegitimate boundaries that separate the "underclass."

The controversial shared-meal included communion or the celebration of the Lord's Table. Imagine the loss to the first century Ekklesia in refusing to share in the celebration of the Lord's death and resurrection with Gentiles.

This controversy exists today among us when we isolate ourselves to only open our homes and tables to other believers, people in our social class, or even to people in our personal "Denomination." How much do we demonstrate the heart of our Lord when we invite the poor and misfits of the world to dine with us or to open our homes to them and become their friends?

Do people call us friends of sinners like they did Lord Jesus? The misfits were drawn to Jesus before, and they are drawn to Him now. If He is manifest in our life, we will find Him attracting people into our life that He wants to reach through us.

Spiritual Gifts

The gifts of the Spirit were in operation among the first century believers and the Holy Spirit is still doing this same thing today.

> "There are diversities of gifts, but the same Spirit.
>
> There are differences of ministries, but the same Lord. And there are diversities of activities, but it is the same God who works all in all.
>
> But the manifestation of the Spirit is given to each one for the profit of all: for to one is given the word of wisdom through the Spirit, to another the word of knowledge through the same Spirit, to another faith by the same Spirit, to another gifts of healing by the same Spirit, to another the working of miracles, to another prophecy, to another discerning of spirits, to another different kinds of tongues, to another the interpretation of tongues. But one and the same Spirit works all these things, distributing to each one individually as He wills." **1 Corinthians 12:4-11**

He works among us to supernaturally gift and enable us to accomplish His will. There are a series of gifts and so many possible ways for Him to manifest them that we cannot simply box the Holy Spirit into a formula or limit ourselves to one thing.

The Spirit of God will manifest gifts beyond our natural understanding. The following list gives us a value-based framework to help us have a frame of reference to experience His movement. The Holy Spirit is pleased when we re-gift what He gives us. He gives freely and expects us to do the same.

This is often an issue of much controversy. Well, of course it is. If the adversary can keep people from trusting God for supernatural ministry, he wins without any effort. If you are opposed to spiritual gifts, you are by default opposing the Holy Spirit and His ministry. The Lord is working in our midst and broadcasting the frequency of Heaven. When we are walking as spiritually minded, He can speak through us, to us and work miracles through us to demonstrate the Kingdom of God.

Spiritual Gifts in Perspective

1. **To Know Something** - Gifts of Revelation (the word of wisdom, the word of knowledge, the discerning of spirits)

2. **To Do Something** - Gifts of Demonstration (faith, the gifts of healing, the working of miracles)

3. **To Speak Something** - Gifts of Inspiration (divers kinds of tongues, interpretation of tongues, prophecy)

The nine gifts of the Spirit are given to edify or build up the Body of Christ. We do not need to put a limitation on the Holy Spirit by limiting Him to our own understanding or context.

When we position ourselves to move into our inheritance of all things, we transcend the limitations of a gift here or there and begin to move in the full manifestation of the ministry of Jesus Christ as His presence and anointing are among us in fullness.

When Jesus is exalted and His Word received, the gifts of the Holy Spirit are present. We may need to work on our awareness, but He is present and active.

Expect God to speak through you and others when gathering and in our daily rhythms of life by and through the Holy Spirit. Be sensitive always to what the Spirit may be doing.

Spiritual Dialogues

> *"Now on the first day of the week, when the disciples came together to break bread, **Paul, ready to depart the next day, spoke to them** and continued his message until midnight. There were many lamps in the upper room where they were gathered together."* **Acts 20:7-8**

The tradition in what are called church meetings follows the common understanding of the exhortation of Paul to Timothy: "Preach the word!"

When we look at the context of preaching in the first century model, it looks nothing like what we know today. The accounts of believers actually speaking to one another or teaching one another when they gathered, caused onlookers to be astonished and view them with awe.

There are two Greek verbs that are commonly translated "preach" in the New Testament: **κηρύσσω (kerusso)** which means, "to announce or proclaim aloud"[68] and **εὐαγγελίζομαι (euangelizomai)** which means, "to bring or announce good news."[69] These words were very seldom used or associated with believers speaking to an audience of believers. This type of communication is evangelistic and outreach oriented so there is definitely a context for this type of preaching.

There is also an every day context for spiritual dialogues in which there is connection and interaction among the participants. This means people are not being talked at as though the speaker is an expert or authority over them, but rather there is a participation and open conversation.

The word conversation is a wonderful way to view believers gathering. Can you imagine a family eating together and everyone has to raise his or her hand to talk? How silly is that? This type of dynamic can make our gatherings very powerful when we remove the formality and expert air of authority.

Participatory Teaching

There is a word that is used often in the context of believers speaking to one another when they gathered or met together: διαλέγομαι **(Dialegomai)**. This word translates to mean, "To converse, discuss, argue, esp. of instructional discourse that frequently includes exchange of opinions." This is where we get our English word dialogue.[70] We can simply call these spiritual conversations.

In **Acts 19:8,** Paul "reasoned" with the Jews in the synagogues, and in **Acts 19:9**, after he left the synagogue, he continued "reasoning" with the disciples who followed him to the hall of Tyrannus.

In **Acts 20:7-10**, Paul "spoke" to believers in Troas.

Dialegomai is used to describe Paul or another believer "discussing" or "arguing" with nonbelievers. In these instances, the verb is usually translated "reason," "argue," or "discuss."

The power of this form of communication is in making connections together. When people distance themselves from a stage and speak <u>at</u> those they are "teaching," it lacks the power of relationship and accountability. The idea that we need an expert over us detracts from gathering in the name of Jesus and expecting Him to manifest His presence in our midst and communicate through His Body.

Leadership

We are moving in the "all things" dynamic of the convergence. God is working all things together for good for those called according to His purpose. We must be completely reliant on the Holy Spirit as He leads us into our inheritance together.

From The Message Translation:

> Now Jesus turned to address his disciples, along with the crowd that had gathered with them. "The religion scholars and Pharisees are competent teachers in God's Law. You won't go wrong in following their teachings on Moses. But be careful about following them. They talk a good line, but they don't live it. They don't take it into their hearts and live it out in their behavior. It's all spit-and-polish veneer.

> "Instead of giving you God's Law as food and drink by which you can banquet on God, they package it in bundles of rules, loading you down like pack animals. They seem to take pleasure in watching you stagger under these loads, and wouldn't think of lifting a finger to help. Their lives are perpetual fashion shows, embroidered prayer shawls one day and flowery prayers the next. They love to sit at the head table at church dinners, basking in the most prominent positions, preening in the radiance of public flattery, receiving honorary degrees, and getting called 'Doctor' and 'Reverend.'

> "Don't let people do that to you, put you on a pedestal like that. **You all have a single Teacher, and you are all classmates.** Don't set people up as experts over your life, letting them tell you what to do. Save that

authority for God; let him tell you what to do. No one else should carry the title of 'Father'; you have only one Father, and He's in heaven. And don't let people maneuver you into taking charge of them. There is only one Life-Leader for you." **Matthew 23:1-12**

With Christ in view, we should call ourselves a learning community. That means we center on Christ as the Teacher. The community relates to one another with the aim of creating an atmosphere or incubator to rapidly mature believers to mobilize and multiply.

Much time and energy in the West is geared towards the extract and disciple model. This can take years to mature a new believer because academic based teaching does not impart life and revelation.

The Lord Himself told us to relate to one another as equals. Not one expert over the other, but rather to one another. **We must ensure we center on THE TEACHER and not A TEACHER.**

Remember, there is no special "teaching anointing" referred to in Scripture. We do, however, each receive a learning anointing. Learning stirs up from inside of us in response to the anointing in us to learn rather than from a special teacher anointing. The process of teaching others is to stir up revelation from within.

The Teacher (Christ) energizes us each to learn from one another through an environment that fosters supernatural learning. Each one of us has the capacity to learn directly from the Spirit inwardly and through others. We can each teach one another as the anointing to learn has been placed in each of us.

> *"But the anointing which you have received from Him abides in you, and you do not need that anyone teach you;"*
> **1 John 2:17**

The one another dynamic is God's plan for ministry. That means the body ministers life and revelation to one another as Christ manifests Himself among us as the Teacher.

Much pressure is put upon pastors and teachers to do all the work of ministry. The pastor and teacher are each equipping ministries given to equip the Body to mature and to function as every part does its share and not to do the ministry for us.

The one another principle is used well over a hundred times in Scripture. As we have said, the teacher's function is to teach people how to learn from the Holy Spirit, not to create a long-term dependence on them as an expert or guru. God can and does speak to us through every member of the Body.

First Followers

People do not generally follow a leader directly. The truth is that until one person begins to follow another there is no leading. Once one person begins to follow the original leader, they become a First Follower. The next followers that come on-board are following the example of the first follower.

This is an exact model of New Testament leadership. We are not leading people to our ministry, our program, or ourselves. We are rather demonstrating, by example, how to follow Christ. We lead others into an encounter with Him.

The idea of there being a hierarchy pyramid from the top down is contrary to the very directive from Jesus about being a servant. When we view the Christ life as a race, we then see that a leader is simply someone either starting early or running faster. They are able to lead by going out ahead and sharing their experience with those coming from behind. Everyone is running on a level playing field.

Leadership: Example Setters

The function of leadership in the Body of Christ is not to control, authorize, or delegate. Those are worldly concepts. Leadership as the world sees it is never taught or mentioned in the New Testament except when the Lord Jesus says don't be a part of that type of authority structure either by lording over others or by letting them lord over you. That simply means that the New Testament model of leadership has nothing to do with "bossing."

> *"And when the ten heard it, they were greatly displeased with the two brothers. But Jesus called them to Himself and said, "You know that the rulers of the Gentiles lord it over them, and those who are great exercise authority over them. Yet it shall not be so among you; but whoever desires to become great among you, let him be your servant. **And whoever desires to be first among you, let him be your slave— just as the Son of Man did not come to be served, but to serve, and to give His life a ransom for many."***
> **Matthew 20:25-28**

The word facilitate or empower is more in line with the way that leadership is modeled in the New Testament. What a different attitude would be adopted if we had servant meetings rather than leadership meetings. The object of leading is to release others and not control them or their resources.

Leadership is not a fast track to the center, the spotlight, the front, or the top. It is becoming a servant to others.

How many people in leadership draw their resources from the people they should be serving? Leading others also means we are sowing into their lives and vision rather than asking them to sow into ours. The Lord can direct them to give, but we should not be teaching them that this is an expected act of obedience.

Empowering Others

- **Encourage others to function rather than "let" them function or giving them tasks.**

- **Invest resources in others rather than use their resources to further our own interests.**

- **Serve others rather than having them serve our vision or submitting to us.**

- **Help others discover God's plan and release them to do it rather than help them find a way to serve our plan or our vision.**

- **Put others in the spotlight and not ourselves!**

Very often there is a belief that leadership means thinking for people and telling people what to do. Even in its most basic use, this principle falls into the idea of "lording over." This is why people believe they are "under people" or that other people are "under them." That is the wrong Kingdom.

The New Testament model of leadership is one of establishing a pattern of faithful living that demonstrates the Kingdom.

It works this way: if you are a leader, then you are under everyone else. Many people seem to have this backward. If Christ is the Foundation, then all the climbing and striving to go higher seems to be moving us in the wrong direction.

> *"Remember your leaders, those who spoke to you the word of God. Consider the outcome of their way of life, and imitate their faith."* **Hebrews 13:7**

> *"Be imitators of me, as I am of Christ."*
> **1 Corinthians 11:1**

What About Fivefold Ministry?

The fivefold gifts are temporary and are necessary until the Body of Christ becomes fully mature in Christ.[71]

> "And He Himself gave some to be apostles, some prophets, some evangelists, and some pastors and teachers for the equipping of the saints for the work of ministry, for the edifying of the body of Christ, **till we all come to the unity of the faith and of the knowledge of the Son of God**, to a perfect man, to the measure of the stature of the fullness of Christ." **Ephesians 4:11-13**

The ultimate goal of fivefold ministry is the maturing and perfecting of the Body of Christ to flow and function as a living spiritual organism. These are not static positions, but are rather spiritual functions with an intended purpose and goal.

Every believer is called to function and minister life.

The Lord's view is for the fivefold ministry to exist only until the Body of Christ reaches full stature. It is at this time that we will be empowered to operate in the full inheritance of sonship. Fivefold ministry should function with the ultimate goal of maturing the saints unto the full stature of the measure of Christ and not to perpetuate a ministry, a job, or an income.

The Holy Spirit was sent to us to cause movement and spiritual enlargement. Joining Him in this mission will bring us to the ultimate fruitfulness of our destiny on this planet.

The work He has given us is relational. It always comes down to relationships based on His working and fitting us together according to His amazing master plan. Our inheritance is the same as the Lord Jesus. It is in the saints. As we mature one another, we are increasing the measure and value of our inheritance. The more we do for others and facilitate their growth, the greater our rewards.

When a new believer is brought into an encounter with and confesses Jesus Christ as Lord, the very next step is to baptize them. At this point, they are now ambassadors of Christ to their family, and it is important that we validate their qualification for ministry based on Christ's righteousness and the power of the Holy Spirit.

They should receive a clear explanation of how to share the gospel and we can help them share their testimony with their extended household.

They are now a follower of Christ, which makes them a first follower leader. They are to begin immediately setting the example of following the indwelling Lordship of Jesus Christ.

Distributed Authority

> *"Then Jesus came to them and said, "All authority in heaven and on earth has been given to me. Therefore go and make disciples of all nations, baptizing them in the name of the Father and of the Son and of the Holy Spirit, and teaching them to obey everything I have commanded you. And **surely I am with you always**, to the very end of the age."*
> **Matthew 28:18-20**

Lord Jesus has sent us into the world to embody His message. The message is not delegated to us to deliver on our own. He delivers it Himself through us as we embody Him.

Just the same, He has not delegated authority to select individuals to run things in His absence. That is contrary to His being the living and effective Head of the Body.

Convergence – Summing Up All Things In Christ

The United States is not a Democracy. It is a Republic. That means that we elect representatives that operate as our delegated authority for a certain time. If they don't break any laws, they remain in office for the full term and cannot be replaced until a new vote is conducted.

Spiritual authority and power are not simply given to us, but are rather distributed as needed. We are not delegates left on our own until the Lord Returns.

The Head (Christ) distributes authority and power, wisdom, and direction through the Body in real-time to accomplish His will. The idea that one person has been delegated position based decision-making power over the lives of others in the Body of Christ is not supported in the New Testament. Such a practice stifles the growth and maturity of others.

In Scripture, there is found a shared leadership model. That means that the more mature or elder in the Lord together make important decisions. Such decisions are not directive, but generally corrective in nature. This creates an atmosphere of accountability as they are also submitting to one another.

We are admonished to submit one to another and not necessarily to yoke ourselves under authority figures. This is a common misunderstanding. When we submit to an authority figure it is bondage. This is not freedom in Christ. When we submit to one another in the body, however, it is empowering.

If someone expects submission because of a position, they are operating from the wrong kingdom. They are seeking to control us or exert an influence from the flesh. That is not Holy Spirit sourced, but is rather religious. This does not minister life.

We submit ourselves by following the example of mature believers. Christ is our Head, and we are all members of Him.

Authority and Fivefold Ministry

"For we are His workmanship, created in Christ Jesus for good works, which God prepared beforehand that we should walk in them.

Therefore remember that you, once Gentiles in the flesh — who are called Uncircumcision by what is called the Circumcision made in the flesh by hands — that at that time you were without Christ, being aliens from the commonwealth of Israel and strangers from the covenants of promise, having no hope and without God in the world. But now in Christ Jesus you who once were far off have been brought near by the blood of Christ.

For He Himself is our peace, who has made both one, and has broken down the middle wall of separation, having abolished in His flesh the enmity, that is, the law of commandments contained in ordinances, so as to create in Himself one new man from the two, thus making peace, and that He might reconcile them both to God in one body through the cross, thereby putting to death the enmity. And He came and preached peace to you who were afar off and to those who were near. For through Him we both have access by one Spirit to the Father.

Now, therefore, you are no longer strangers and foreigners, but fellow citizens with the saints and members of the household of God, **having been built on the foundation of the apostles and prophets, Jesus Christ Himself being the chief cornerstone, in whom the whole building, being fitted together, grows into a holy temple in the Lord, in whom you also are being built together for a dwelling place of God in the Spirit."** **Ephesians 2:10-30**

The work is already finished and we are now walking out God's plan. Just as the citizens of the USA refer to the work of the Founding Fathers, we look to the finished work of the apostles and prophets as the foundation of the household. This is again the use of the oikos principle and not a religious institution or organization. The Lord is building a household, not a "church."

While we value the work of the apostle and prophets today, the Scripture says we are members of a household that has been built on a foundation that has already been set. For example, the early believers in **Acts Chapter 2** gathered to enjoy the "apostles teaching." Our advantage in this matter is that they wrote it down for us in letters. Each of us has access to the same apostles teaching today through the New Testament letters written to the Body of Christ. There is no new foundation to be laid. By faith, we must take hold of what is already there.

The term apostle comes from the term apostolos in Greek. It was a term used by the Romans for one who was sent into a conquered territory to establish the new ekklesia.

> *"The stone the builders rejected has become the capstone;*
> *the Lord has done this, and it is marvelous in our eyes."*
> **Matthew 21:42**

Christ is shown both as the chief cornerstone and as the capstone. The Chief Cornerstone is the plum line or prototype that God uses to measure. The work of the capstone is to bind everything together. The work of apostles and prophets then is to simply ensure the Body is functioning organically according to the measure of Christ.

The simple way to view this is that the fivefold ministry is like a maintenance man. The object is to ensure that the Body is functioning correctly. This might require some adjustments now and then, but when things are working smoothly, the maintenance man should be functioning as an equal member of the body and supplying life to the interconnected parts.

Paul stated that his authority was for building up. The Lord Jesus said if we want to be first, that is achieved by becoming a slave. That is a strong word: slave.

We cannot effectively be a slave and boss at the same time. So following Paul's example would place the **Ephesians 4:11** fivefold ministries not as bosses, but servants given to the Body of Christ for equipping all for ministry.

Equipping could be seen like armor bearing. In ancient times, an armor bearer was a servant who worked for the knight and not the other way around. This could not be any clearer than that.

"For even if I should boast somewhat more about our authority, which the Lord gave us for edification and not for your destruction, I shall not be ashamed—lest I seem to terrify you by letters." **2 Corinthians 10:8**

*"But Jesus called them to Himself and said, "You know that the rulers of the Gentiles lord it over them, and those who are great exercise authority over them. Yet it shall not be so among you; but whoever desires to become great among you, let him be your servant. **And whoever desires to be first among you, let him be your slave**— just as the Son of Man did not come to be served, but to serve, and to give His life a ransom for many."* **Matthew 20:25-28**

Professional Ministers and Laity

The idea that there are special classes of believers who are either "more called" or "more holy" is not supported in Scripture. We are all called to ministry as a royal priesthood. This is a living function of our birthright and not a profession.

As we have seen there are the fivefold equipping ministries. These are not professional positions that must be filled, but rather they are spiritual functions and giftings.

Convergence – Summing Up All Things In Christ

The power of the Ekklesia is the obvious and powerful leading and presence of Jesus Christ through the Spirit.

Many people are willing to just pay professionals to do all their spiritual thinking and ministry. This is usually put upon a single pastor. They expect him to inquire of God for them, pray for them, and make their decisions. We will never mature as a Body with this model of living.

Israel refused to have God as their king and wanted a man to rule over them and it did not go well.

> "Nevertheless the people refused to obey the voice of Samuel; and they said, 'No, but we will have a king over us, that we also may be like all the nations, and t hat our king may judge us and go out before us and fight our battles.'"
> **1 Samuel 8:19-20**

The issue revealed in Hebrews is that we should be maturing to function in our priesthood. When the Scripture says we should be teaching, the Holy Spirit is saying we each should be going and making disciples. This is our birthright and not a job.

> *"For though by this time you ought to be teachers, you need someone to teach you again the first principles of the oracles of God; and you have come to need milk and not solid food. For everyone who partakes only of milk is unskilled in the word of righteousness, for he is a babe. But solid food belongs to those who are of full age, that is, those who by reason of use have their senses exercised to discern both good and evil."* **Hebrews 5:12-14**

Only babies and animals need to be fed. We are to be maturing in the Spirit so we can each fulfill our function as a royal priesthood and draw upon resources to release to others. What is often called "going to church to get fed," is really just a lot of milk drinking. We will never mature to eating solid food as spiritual adults until we exercise our spiritual senses. This requires us to take responsibility for our place in the Body and to function at full capacity by yielding our bodies and ourselves to Christ for His use.

> *"Let no one cheat you of your reward, taking delight in false humility and worship of angels, intruding into those things which he has not seen, vainly puffed up by his fleshly mind, and not holding fast to the Head, from whom all the body, nourished and knit together by joints and ligaments, grows with the increase that is from God."* **Colossians 2:18-19**

> *"Now the Lord is the Spirit; and where the Spirit of the Lord is, there is liberty."* **2 Corinthians 3:17**

Romans 13 tell us that God is ultimately orchestrating all authority structures. There is no question that as followers of Jesus Christ and sons of God that we respect and submit to authority.

We don't lord over other believers and expect them to submit to us as delegated authorities. **It is impossible to read the clear words of our Lord Jesus Christ on the matter and perceive that we are in charge of others.** We are told to submit to one another and never to lord over others. That is how relational Kingdom authority works. We submit to the example of those who demonstrate the heart of Jesus Christ by laying their lives down for others.

Much damage has occurred through authority movements in the past. We must learn from that and not let ownership over others quench the fire of the Holy Spirit. We will see God do amazing exploits in the harvest as the end of the ages draws near. The first century believers were looked upon with awe because of the love demonstrated in their communities. This love makes the Kingdom tangible for the world to see.

Chapter Five
Multiplication

"Then the word of God spread, and the number of the disciples multiplied greatly in Jerusalem, and a great many of the priests were obedient to the faith." **Acts 6:7**

"Then He said to them, 'The harvest truly is great, but the laborers are few; therefore pray the Lord of the harvest to send out laborers into His harvest.'" **Luke 10:2**

"But the word of God grew and multiplied." **Acts 12:24**

"Now a certain woman named Lydia heard us. She was a seller of purple from the city of Thyatira, who worshiped God. The Lord opened her heart to heed the things spoken by Paul." **Luke 16:14**

Intentional Gospel

> *"God, who at various times and in various ways spoke in time past to the fathers by the prophets, has in these last days spoken to us by His Son."* **Hebrews 1:1**

Living as a community in the convergence means we are constantly moving with the stream of God's will in the Spirit. We do not have to add to our schedule any extra ministry or spiritual activities in order to bring forth the ministry of reconciliation and redemption. We live our lives with gospel intentionality in everything we do. Our ministry is to yield to the Holy Spirit as He reveals Christ in and through our lives.

> *"Just as He chose us in Him before the foundation of the world, that we should be holy and without blame before Him in love."* **Ephesians 1:4**

The Lord did not choose you or me individually before the foundation of the world. **He chose <u>US</u> together in <u>HIM</u>!**

Evangelism is commonly considered to be a soul winning exercise and is seen as something embarrassing or awkward for new and experienced believers. It is also presented as something we must go and do outside of our normal activities.

While the Holy Spirit can direct specific outreaches, we can also experience tremendous results while living in the rest of His finished purpose. **Ephesians 2:10** tells us we were created "in Christ Jesus" for good works which He prepared beforehand for us to walk in.

Christ is the new creation factory in which God creates us. He handpicked us in Him before the foundation of the world. Understand that He is not creating you and me but in Christ, He has already created us as a multi-member image. We are coming into a destiny that was prepared before the foundation of the world. It is a mutual destiny prepared for us.

Much teaching on evangelism focuses on seeking out individuals to make a decision for Christ either directly or through large outreach efforts. The goal is to achieve a prayer or an altar call. There is nothing wrong with this model of ministry. **We are working in a dimension that shares the good news through people, rather than towards them.**

When living in the convergence, we learn to see the framework of existing relationships God intends to reach and to find the very bridges or "people of peace" that God chose before the foundation of the world.

We don't need to focus on winning the world, but rather we simply align ourselves with the ancient pathway God has ordained for us that leads to the people God is already preparing to believe. We will be referring to them as a "person of peace."

We will examine the pattern demonstrated by the Lord Jesus in His sending of the twelve and the seventy and the protocols He established for them. This same pattern can be found through the accounts recorded by Luke in the Book of Acts.

The object of discovering God's pattern is not to set up an ABC or 123-step program. Rather, we can see a value and principle based framework that empowers us to see who, where, and how the Holy Spirit is working and join Him. When the Spirit leads us, we enjoy a 100% success rate. The results belong to Him. We simply follow the instructions.

This may require us to strip off tradition and put on our "Son Glasses" so we can see what God is doing.

The Household

God's Relational Framework

Exodus 12 is a very powerful example of God's intention to save entire households. When the blood of the lamb was placed on the door, it impacted everyone inside. The Lord said, **"When I see the blood, I will pass over."** These same Israelites were very quick to grumble and doubt even in the middle of signs and wonders. God was not looking at their faith as a whole, but rather each household was saved because He was looking at the blood on the doors of all who obeyed.

When operating outside of an organization or in a persecuted territory, "underground" oikos work as a relational framework. This enables us to see progress and measure our sphere of influence or authority. Many people say they do not know God's will for their life or ministry. The oikos ministry process is for every one of us. It is the Holy Spirit's method of reaching the harvest field. We can use this process to move beyond an organized or institutional paradigm and begin operating from an apostolic relational paradigm.

Oikos communities are featured at the end of nearly every one of the epistles addressed to the ekklesia or churches of various cities. In a very broad account in **Romans 16** Paul addresses different oikos and greets numerous ekklesia that gathered in different oikos. He repeatedly uses the term ekklesia to reference these households and communities of faith. Romans 16 is written to numerous households:

> **The household (oikos) of Priscilla and Aquila (v.4-5)**
>
> **The household (oikos) of Aristobulus (v.10)**

The household (oikos) of Narcissus (v.11)

Verse 14 says, "Greet Asyncritus, Phlegon, Hermes, Patrobas, Hermas and the brothers with them." A community, with the term "brothers" (adelphous) or a similar term for ekklesia or oikos. And greet Philologus, Julia, Nereus and his sister, and Olympas all the saints with them."

When we move our focus from trying to reach one person at a time to, "get them saved" and align with the oikos process, we move into a place of leverage and multiplication. Once we identify the "person of peace," we have a lighthouse for the gospel in which the light and glory of the gospel of Jesus Christ can be seen.

How much more attractive are supernaturally transformed families than programs, presentations, and cathedral type of experiences? Bringing Christ into context in people's lives and cultural dynamics affords us incredible opportunities to reach people that would never step foot into a modern church service.

Discipling Existing Networks

Existing social networks can be discipled and our assignment is not necessarily to break up what is already in place by extracting people. We need not re-create new social networks and families, but can rather bring Jesus into context and therefore kingdomize/disciple what already exists.

The object is to infiltrate enemy territory with a message from our home world. Remember that rogue forces from this same world have taken control of the world system, and have control of the motives and behaviors of unregenerate humans.

The Holy Spirit prepares the heart of family leaders to hear the Gospel and to receive Him. In a western context, family bonds are not as tight as we see in eastern cultures. This began during the industrial revolution when families became smaller consumer based units. We need to adapt to this context and seek wisdom and direction from the Holy Spirit in respect to modern group dynamics.

Expect and Watch For People of Peace

We should expect the Holy Spirit to order our steps in such a way that people are being prepared for us before we meet them and be open to finding "persons of peace" often and everywhere. Our natural thinking will not always be able to understand what God is doing. In **Acts 10**, Cornelius, for example, was a professional soldier. Also, the Phillipian jailer of **Acts 16** was torturing Paul and Silas and even put their feet in stocks prior to the earthquake.

We position ourselves for some amazing surprises when we remain flexible to new contexts and are flexible to the Holy Spirit's thought on the who and the where of the ministry. It took a special revelation from the Holy Spirit for Peter to see the Lord's plan to share the gospel with Gentiles within their own cultural context. This required a direct intervention in Peter's imagination to expand his ability to understand the work of the Holy Spirit outside of his current frame of reference.

In order to mobilize believers to use relational networks, the first thing we must realize is that evangelism is not a program.

Oikos based evangelism is not some kind of program that you start, but is a framework that allows us to see where and how the Holy Spirit is working and align with Him. It is a supernatural process that taps into the way society has functioned and operated for thousands of years..

Methods and programs that require work and natural planning have replaced the simplicity and power of the network based oikos evangelism. If it seems like work, it is probably a human giftedness based model.

Oikos evangelism is a process that builds on the natural "webs" of relationships, which exist in every person's life and can energize us to find the people whose heart God is already working with. **The multiplication dynamic occurs because the Lord is already working on the hearts of their social networks.** Part of making disciples is to teach them how to tap into this dimension of discipleship and kingdom building by being able to see where God is already working in their family's and friend's lives.

We are not trying to look for something to do or someone to talk with about our faith. We are rather moving into a stream of relational power as our Father wills in which He is already operating and working. Oikos evangelism is a "social system based on common kinship, common community and common interests and is not only Trans cultural but Trans historical as well, reaching across centuries."[72]

Households Central Framework of Gospel

The oikos played a central role in the spread of the gospel in the first century. The Lord Jesus would capture a person's heart and this would powerfully affect the others in the household network.

Since these household networks were relationally connected, the gospel was spread from household to household like a virus. A virus is usually spread through an entire household.

Multiplication

Households Were Missional Centers For The Gospel

Once an oikos became centered on Jesus as Lord and Savior, this oikos became the center for ministry and disciple making for the surrounding community. This oikos would grow and multiply as new believers from outside the original household network joined them.

This same model works well for us today in city-centric movements. We start by opening the home for ministry and expand to the surrounding neighborhood and out to the city.

Christ Centered Multiplying Oikos

The Holy Spirit is working through Christ-centered multiplying oikos. These supernatural powered Christ-centered networks of relationships break through class, gender, race and cultural barriers by creating a new common ground in Christ by the power and will of the Holy Spirit.

The Lord was always intentional and moving in a prophetic stream of the Father's will. The encounters He had with people were always for a specific purpose. When He engaged people on a personal level, it was usually to engage them to become a bridge to their OIKOS.

In **Mark 5:19** the man delivered from a legion of demons is told to go back to his oikos to tell what great things the Lord had done for him. He went from terrorizing a region to being an evangelist in one day.

In the case of both Levi **Mark 2:15-17** and Zacchaeus **Luke 19:9** they gather their close associates around them to be with the Lord.

John 4:39 has a great example with the Samaritan woman that had been divorced several times bringing her whole territory to see Jesus and after the healing of the official's son his whole oikos believes: **John 4:53**

John 1 shows more natural connections as Andrew brings his brother Peter to the Lord **(1:41)** and Philip brings Nathaniel **(1:45).**

Intentionally Raising Up Laborers

We look to the Lord's example to develop an intentional plan and strategy for using these principles as value based frameworks. When sharing the gospel with an individual we explain the ministry of reconciliation and call the person to action on behalf of their family and friends.

When we are sharing the GLOCAL vision with new believers and the reality that the world is under the sway of the wicked one, their obvious response should be concern for their friends and family. This is different from an attraction-based focus on personal salvation and classroom teaching.

If we are to do evangelism the way Jesus did, we need to be moving in the stream of the Father's will and keep our "Son Glasses" on to see who He is arranging us to meet. We then bring them into an encounter with Jesus so that He can reveal Himself through them to their oikos.

We are looking for laborers, not spectators or seat fillers. These are people through whom God is already preparing and planning for more laborers to be raised up through their already existing relationships.

Apostolic Protocols
God's Social Networking

There is an apostolic prototype in the sending of the seventy by the Lord Jesus. He revealed a strategy that is value based and really quite simple.

Keep in mind that the key to Spirit Led Ministry is to be intentional about our schedule and to see our home, job, and other social atmospheres as platforms for hospitality and ministry.

✓ **Pray**
✓ **Go**
✓ **Bless**
✓ **Expect**

When our schedule belongs to God our days can be filled with "persons of peace."

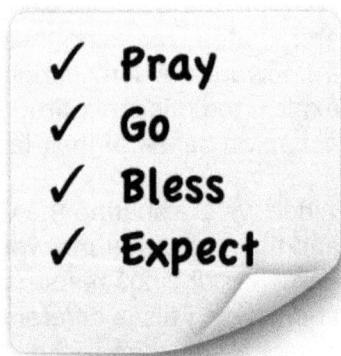

The Kingdom of God Is At Hand

The Great Commission of Matthew 28 tells us to make disciples, "As we go" As we go in the same way as Jesus and his disciples, our life, words and actions announce that the Kingdom of God is at hand. The message makes sense because it is demonstrated in our lives.

"But whatever house you enter, first say, 'Peace to this house.' And if a son of peace is there, your peace will rest on it; if not, it will return to you." **(Luke 10:5-6)** We are also to find the "worthy man" **(Matthew 10:11)** or the "son of peace" **(Luke 10:6)** and use that home as a base of operations or an embassy for the Kingdom in the community.

Strategy 1 - Pray For Laborers

> *"The harvest truly is great, but the laborers are few; therefore* **pray the Lord of the harvest to send out laborers into His harvest."** **Luke 10:1**

There is no direct commandment to pray for the lost. We are rather instructed to pray for laborers!

The word used in Greek for sending out laborers is the same one used for casting out demons: "ekballô." It is usually translated as "casting out." Ekballô is used 34 times for the casting out of demons and once for throwing out the moneychangers in the Temple.

The Lord is going to launch us out like stretching a rubber band and shoot us into the harvest.

When we use core values as a container and this simple strategy, there is plenty of room for flexibility and Spirit led success. The key value of this powerful process is to remember that the Holy Spirit initiates this process. He is ready to launch some laborers.

The most important thing is to follow Him and not rely on a pattern or some technique. As we sow into this principle with action, we can expect to experience the multiplying of the Body of Christ.

Strategy 2 - Go where the Holy Spirit is moving

> *"After this the Lord appointed seventy-two others and sent them two by two ahead of Him to every town and place where He was about to go"* **Luke 10:1**

Jesus appointed the seventy-two and sent them out. They went ahead to prepare the places He was going to go into Himself.

In our current season, the Holy Spirit is the One going. It makes no sense to stay where we are if He is going somewhere else. We need to ask Him where He is going and join in.

> *"Now when they had gone through Phrygia and the region of Galatia, they were forbidden by the Holy Spirit to preach the word in Asia.*
>
> *After they had come to Mysia, they tried to go into Bithynia, but the Spirit did not permit them.*
>
> *So passing by Mysia, they came down to Troas. And a vision appeared to Paul in the night. A man of Macedonia stood and pleaded with him, saying, Come over to Macedonia and help us. Now after he had seen the vision, immediately we sought to go to Macedonia, concluding that the Lord had called us to preach the gospel* to them." **Acts 16:6-10**
>
> *"When you enter a town and are not welcomed, go into its streets and say, 'Even the dust of your town that sticks to our feet we wipe off against you. Yet be sure of this: The kingdom of God is at hand.'"* **Luke 10:10-11**

The stakes are high, and our attention needs to be focused where we will bear fruit for our time. We can be sure that if we are not welcome, we are not getting full benefit of our time.

Strategy 3 - Bless The Person of Peace

Identifying the person of peace is a process of being intentional and expecting the Lord to show them to you.. Every person of peace testimony is going to be unique to the situation. We are simply using a framework of Scriptural principles to position us to see and know where the Lord is working. When we are intentional and pray for God to reveal the person of peace, we will position ourselves to discover them.

Finding people of peace is about being in harmony with the Lord and moving with His rhythm. It is the fruit of a constant expectant relationship and not something you can get reading about it or attending classes. You can read about splitting the atom, but until you actually do it, you are not an atomic scientist. The value based strategy is that we know it is His will to reveal them so we ask Him to make it clear who the person is and to be specific.

Remember that we are moving in the rest of God. He has a plan and He will reveal with whom and where He is working as we position ourselves to listen and to expect Him to show us.

We are His workmanship and He is building us up together into His dwelling place. Each stone has a specific place and function according to His eternal purpose. The ultimate goal is for His image to be formed. This requires us to be plugged into the Author Himself as He walks us through the plan.

Releasing Peace

How many people do you know that have ever once done this? We can assure you it works by experience and because it is instructed and demonstrated by the Lord.

We can do this before entering an establishment. Simply ask the Lord what He intends for the people inside and without drawing attention test the spiritual climate saying, "The kingdom of God is at hand" or "Peace unto this house" and watch to see what happens. This simple act of faith and obedience releases faith into the atmosphere and exerts spiritual dominion over the spiritual unseen realm.

The releasing of peace could be as simple as sharing the gospel of peace, or simply saying a blessing in the name of the Lord. It is simply a matter of making Jesus the potential for conversation. It doesn't mean we necessarily start preaching the gospel, but rather just open the conversation. The key is to be sensitive to what the Holy Spirit is telling you to do. He knows the perfect way to bridge the conversation.

This priestly blessing approach opens the door to a prophetic discussion. That means that the spiritual gifts can be activated and we can begin to receive supernatural knowledge as the Holy Spirit reveals His will in the matter.

Focus on people who are interested in hearing about Jesus, rather than convincing them to listen. This is why joining the Holy Spirit where He is already working is so important. This is the meaning of being intentional in making disciples. With this in mind, finding people and houses of peace and then making disciples, is simply finding ways to bring Jesus into focus.

How do we make Jesus the focus? Ask Him what He wants to say and trust Him to speak through our thoughts and our words. Jesus said his words were spirit and life and we have the same anointing within us. We should expect our words to vibrate with the frequency of Heaven.

> "After this the Lord appointed seventy-two others and sent them two by two ahead of Him to every town and place where He was about to go. He told them,... When you enter a house, first say, 'Peace to this house.' If a man of peace is there, your peace will rest on him; if not, it will return to you."
> **Luke 10:1,2,5-6**

We need not be overly concerned with locations. The subversive power of the gospel is such that we need to become open to operating anywhere and everywhere for the sake of the gospel. We may be surprised at the places and people God can send us to that we may never have even noticed before.

Keep in mind that when Jesus is speaking about releasing

peace on the house, He means oikos. **The peace is to rest upon people not places.** He gave similar protocols when He sent out the twelve.

> *"Now whatever city or town you enter, inquire who in it is worthy, and stay there till you go out. And when you go into a household, greet it. If the household is worthy, let your peace come upon it. But if it is not worthy, let your peace return to you."* **Matthew 10:11-13**

Expectation Births Awareness

Expecting and watching for the Holy Spirit to lead us to a "worthy person" keeps us intentional in our schedule and releases a dimension of faith that pleases the Lord. He will meet your faith with one opportunity after another and fill your life with His resources for others.

Finding The Person of Peace

Did the Holy Spirit direct you to them?

Did they approach you?

Are they receptive to you when you reveal you are a "Jesus Person?"

Are they willing to talk about spiritual matters?

Are they a person of influence?

Have they declared Jesus Christ is Lord?

Are they willing to be baptized in view of their family and/or friends?

Paul's Strategy

From The Message Translation:

> "They went to Phrygia, and then on through the region of Galatia. Their plan was to turn west into Asia province, but the Holy Spirit blocked that route. So they went to Mysia and tried to go north to Bithynia, but the Spirit of Jesus wouldn't let them go there either. Proceeding on through Mysia, they went down to the seaport Troas.
>
> That night Paul had a dream: A Macedonian stood on the far shore and called across the sea. 'Come over to Macedonia and help us!' The dream gave Paul his map. We went to work at once getting things ready to cross over to Macedonia. All the pieces had come together. We knew now for sure that God had called us to preach the good news to the Europeans." **Acts 16:6-10**

This is the power of moving in the convergence of God's will. He will guide and direct us to the specific people and relationships He has prepared for us. We can trust Him and His timing to guide us to the correct place and time for others to experience the Lord Jesus.

This is the **GPS – Glory Positioning System** in action. God has already planned this out and has resources and people lined up for us as we walk His plan.

The resources we need are already en route and in place. Here is the Lord showing how He moved in this awareness:

> "Go into the village opposite you, and immediately you will find a donkey tied, and a colt with her. Loose them and bring them to Me." **Matthew 21:2**
>
> " Nevertheless, lest we offend them, go to the sea, cast in a hook, and take the fish that comes up first. And when you

have opened its mouth, you will find a piece of money; take that and give it to them for Me and you." **Matthew 17:27**

Paul most often went directly to the local synagogue to identify his target person of influence. There appeared to be no synagogue in Macedonia so they discerned where God was working:

> *"And on the Sabbath day we went out of the city to the riverside, where prayer was customarily made; and we sat down and spoke to the women who met there. Now a certain woman named Lydia heard us. She was a seller of purple from the city of Thyatira, who worshiped God. The Lord opened her heart to heed the things spoken by Paul. And when she and her household were baptized, she begged us, saying, "If you have judged me to be faithful to the Lord, come to my house and stay. So she persuaded us."* **Acts 16:13-15**

Lydia was the person of peace and influence and the first convert in Philippi. Paul and Barnabas established a church in her house.

Sometimes the person of peace or influence can be a local official or key community leader.

Publius, the chief official of Malta welcomed Paul into his home **(Acts 28:7)**. Lydia was a successful businesswoman. In Paphos, the proconsul, Sergius Paulus, sent for Barnabas and Saul because he wanted to hear the word of God **(Acts 13:6-7)**.

Bringing a person with significant influence into an encounter with Christ can be a catalyst to launch the whole neighborhood or city into a Christ-centered movement.

Healing the Sick

Once a new person of peace has been born of the Spirit, we should expect there to be opportunities to heal the sick.
Luke recorded Paul praying for Publius's sick father. **(Acts 28:8-10).**

When people hear about the healing, they will be interested and curious to see for themselves. This is the demonstration of the Word. Some may come along wanting to be healed and will end up believing the gospel and as they encounter the Lord. This can be the result of physical and emotional healing. Again, ask the Holy Spirit what He has planned and expect signs and wonders to follow.

Signs are not leading us, but rather signs are following us! The Lord said signs and wonders would follow those who believe: **(Mark 16:17).**

If the miracle is substantial, the Lord could draw a crowd. This opens the door for declaring the gospel and praying for the sick. The Holy Spirit will confirm the preaching with signs and wonders. This was often the pattern seen in the ministry of the Lord Jesus and the disciples:

> *"And they went out and preached everywhere, the Lord working with them and confirming the word through the accompanying signs. Amen."* **Mark 16:20**

Baptism

It is important to bring new believers into an immediate encounter with obedience through baptism. When sharing the gospel and leading new believers to Christ, we should prayerfully encourage them to be baptized as instructed by the Lord:

*"Then Jesus came to them and said, 'All authority in heaven and on earth has been given to me. **Therefore go and make disciples of all nations, baptizing them** in the name of the Father and of the Son and of the Holy Spirit, and teaching them to obey everything I have commanded you. And surely I am with you always, to the very end of the age.'"*
Matthew 28:18-20

There is a section of this book addressing the prophetic power of immediate baptism and the acceleration of the transformation process of Christ-centered communities. Remember, it is the disciple maker that is commanded to go and baptize. The command is given to us to initiate this process on behalf of the new believer. It is not a doctrinal issue.

If you share the gospel of Jesus with someone and they confess Him as Lord and then decline baptism, is He really their Lord? That is quite a test of someone's understanding of lordship. This cannot be accomplished in a parking lot and requires us to be serious and intentional when engaging people to believe in and receive the Lord Jesus Christ.

Baptism of The Holy Spirit

Paul addresses this issue perfectly. We can follow his example as he brought new disciples into an encounter with the Holy Spirit. What better way to see the power of this blessing than to read about Paul's example?

From The Message Translation:

"Now, it happened that while Apollos was away in Corinth, Paul made his way down through the mountains, came to Ephesus, and happened on some disciples there. The first thing he said was, 'Did you receive the Holy Spirit when you believed? Did you take God into your mind only, or did you also embrace him with your heart? Did he get inside you?'

'We've never even heard of that—a Holy Spirit? God within us?'

'How were you baptized, then,' asked Paul.

'In John's baptism.'

'That explains it,' said Paul. "John preached a baptism of radical life-change so that people would be ready to receive the One coming after him, who turned out to be Jesus. If you've been baptized in John's baptism, you're ready now for the real thing, for Jesus.'

And they were. As soon as they heard of it, they were baptized in the name of the Master Jesus. Paul put his hands on their heads and the Holy Spirit entered them. From that moment on, they were praising God in tongues and talking about God's actions. Altogether there were about twelve people there that day." **Acts 19:2-7**

Establishing Kingdom Embassies

The next step is to equip the new believers and teach them to disciple one another through the power of the Holy Spirit. They can even begin gathering together as an Ekklesia, based in the home of the person of peace. The new Oikos-Ekklesia will become a community in which the life of Christ is visibly manifested. As households are brought into the power of Christ, others will be drawn into this community. This is the power of the relational dynamic of oikos evangelism.
There will be a new excitement as fresh prophetic testimonies are shared among the new extended household of God. Fresh believers are a powerful force and have a natural or supernaturally birthed child-like excitement.

When a gathering community gets to be over 15-20 people, it is pregnant and ready to multiply. The object of an oikos movement is not to build large sized communities, but rather to multiply effectively sized mobile, relational and duplicatable communities.

The idea is to maintain a personal dynamic. Once a group starts growing beyond this point, people can get lost in the space dynamic as it moves from personal to social.

Summary of the Oikos Strategy

- **Go where the Holy Spirit is moving.**
- **Seek the person of peace.**
- **Get established in a house.**
- **Heal the sick.**
- **Preach the gospel.**
- **Make disciples.**
- **Baptize new believers.**
- **Establish a community.**
- **Train believers to make disciples.**
- **Baptism of Spirit.**
- **Ordain all believers for ministry.**
- **Expect multiplication.**
- **15-20 people may mean multiplication time.**

Launching Oikos
Catalyzing Subversive Movements

The objective is to launch a movement by following the example of the first century believers. This is only a mission-oriented suggested framework. Ask the Lord for specific direction. Remember, He has this planned out already. We are simply walking out an ancient relational pathway that He prepared us for before the foundation of the world.

The protocols Jesus used shows it only takes two people to get moving. The resources and laborers will quickly materialize in the harvest. This includes servant leaders rising up among the existing relational networks or oikos.

The objective here is to light a relational fire of community and mobilize new believers to become laborers in the harvest. We do not call this church planting because this is the on an in-the-field strategy to multiply the Body of Christ through easily duplicatable, mobile and Spirit led frameworks. Extended households are the relational structure rather than buildings.

To train others, we find that conducting meetings and training in normal everyday locations or "third places" helps new believers to see themselves able to duplicate the process. If we take people to a neutral place or even a "church building" it fosters the extraction mindset. When meeting and training in coffee shops, homes, and other normal places, the opportunity for onlookers and others passing by opens the door for immediate growth and multiplication.

Ask the Lord for a co-laborer and follow His lead in seeking the person of peace.

Tools Needed:

1. Bible
2. Holy Spirit

The Framework is Existing Social Networks

Using the bridge or person of peace model, ask the Holy Spirit to show you the person and start in their home or wherever the Spirit directs. This is the protocol of the seventy found in Luke Chapter 10.

Start With New Believers

Our objective is not really to reshuffle the current pool of believers. Starting a mission-oriented community from newly formed believers turns their extended household (oikos) into a mission field. Fresh transformed lives are a powerful testimony and will be reproductive and infectious to the community. The point is to position people to be captured in the love of Christ and to bring the Kingdom into their network of relationships.

Empower and Release Immediately

Encourage the ministry to be conducted by the new believers and teach them to do the same thing as they multiply. When we instill the expectation for people to be mobilized right at the start, they will be more fruitful in their new life.

Let Scripture Speak

The New Testament was written directly to the Body of Christ. Encourage new believers to gather to read the New Testament out loud together trusting the Holy Spirit to speak. This is a relational and, mobile and duplicatable model.

Headship

Encourage and instruct the new believers to experience the manifest presence of Christ as both Source and Head of their community.

Baptize New Believers

The first step commanded by Lord Jesus in making disciples is to baptize them in the name of the Father, Son and Holy Spirit. As we do this with new believers, we encourage them to do the same. Consider going to their house and make it a prophetic testimony to their household. Most importantly, ask the Lord for His plan.

Filled With The Spirit

Lay hands on new believers and expect them to be filled with the Spirit. It's really that simple.[73]

Multiplication

Encourage multiplication. Sow into the new community the need to mature, expand and multiply to facilitate bringing others in the community into the redeeming power of the Lord Jesus Christ.

Accountability

Don't keep secrets. Be transparent with one another.

Testimony

A new believer is a tremendous resource to their existing relational network. Their transformation and excitement is going to speak very powerfully in the lives of others that know them.

We can teach new believers to share their testimony using Paul's model **Acts 26:1-32:**

1. Before Christ
2. Encounter Story
3. Fresh Transparent Testimony

The key is that the Holy Spirit is the guide in this. Follow His lead and He will give you a 100% success rate. The results are up to Him. We just do what He tells us and we are successful on our end.

Mobile Duplicatable Gatherings

There is no formula for gatherings. The following is a suggested list. Simply pray and ask the Lord what He wants to do individually and collectively. Consciously acknowledge and relate to the Lord and develop the awareness that He is actually present. Invite Him to lead and reveal Himself to the gathering.

Gathering In His Name

> *"For where two or three are gathered together in My name, I am there in the midst of them."* **Matthew 18:20**

Keep attention centered on Christ. Talk to the Lord and defer to Him as the One in charge of the gathering and seek to discern His will and guidance.

1. Praise, Worship and Serious Celebration
2. Celebrate Communion – Bread and Wine
   "For as often as you eat this bread and drink this cup, you proclaim the Lord's death till He comes." **1 Corinthians 1:26**
3. Edifying, exhorting and comforting 'one another'
4. Sharing spiritual gifts and laying on of hands

5. Sharing testimonies, dreams, visions & prophecies etc.
6. Sharing meals is a powerful ministry platform.
7. Intercession for the city and the nations
8. Read Scripture out loud to one another.
9. Leaders don't do everything. They make sure everyone has an opportunity to participate and **no one person dominates. (Do not center on one person or expert.)**
10. Expect the Holy Spirit to speak and to hand out assignments for both in and out of gatherings.

The place of leadership in these gatherings is to facilitate and empower. That means the leader is not doing everything, making all the decisions, or deciding who should talk. Try to refrain from talking directly to the leader or host or raising your hand. Otherwise, things begin to filter through them.

The primary focus of the leader is to insure everyone is comfortable, no one is dominating the time, and everyone is free to participate. If someone is saying something in error, the more mature can help bring things into order.

> *"How is it then, brethren? Whenever you come together, each of you has a psalm, has a teaching, has a tongue, has a revelation, has an interpretation. Let all things be done for edification."* **1 Corinthians 14:26**

The Holy Spirit will use each of us and it can be amazing. We do not all have the same skill level in singing. Picture your Father watching His children perform for Him. We may not be impressed with what someone else is doing in the natural, but God is enjoying it like a loving Dad (Abba).[74]

Missional Accountability

Our gatherings can have an empowerment when we hold one another accountable. This is as simple as submitting one to another. The easiest way to be defeated is to keep secrets and deal with things in the dark.

> *"This is the message which we have heard from Him and declare to you, that God is light and in Him is no darkness at all. If we say that we have fellowship with Him, and walk in darkness, we lie and do not practice the truth.*
>
> *But if we walk in the light as He is in the light, we have fellowship with one another, and the blood of Jesus Christ His Son cleanses us from all sin. If we say that we have no sin, we deceive ourselves, and the truth is not in us. If we confess our sins, He is faithful and just to forgive us our sins and to cleanse us from all unrighteousness."* **1 John 2:5-9**

The object here is to empower one another to hit the mark of God's will for our lives. The enemy works in the dark and God works in the light of fellowship. We are in this process together.

Here is the powerful question we should be asking in our gatherings:

"What is God saying to you and what are you doing about it?

This question can be specific to the moment or in a general sense. The question encourages community accountability by aligning us with God's proceeding Word and will for us.*

* This powerful strategy was introduced to us by 3DM Ministires.

Citywide Convergence

There is a culture shift when 20% or more of a population is impacted. The 80/20 rule has shown that 20% of people impact the behavior of the remaining 80%.[75]

It takes a convergence of many streams to become a river of God's purpose. The object is not in building one church or organization, but in catalyzing a movement. A catalyst launches something and releases it to gather momentum. It's not about ownership or control, but a faith filled advancing of God's Kingdom and not our own. It's like lighting a fire in a field as the wind picks it up and the fire takes on a life of its own. That's the Convergence of God's will and the various streams moving in the wind of the Holy Spirit.

This requires a return to the subversive strategy used by the Lord Jesus. He created movement by operating outside the constrains and rules of organized religion. He invested in one person at a time and released them to their purpose. In order to light a fire in the fields of harvest we must be out in the field starting heart fires and not inside a building waiting on the harvest to come to us. The wind and other forces will quickly take it out of our control to become a wild fire of the Holy Spirit. That is being a catalyst. When the fire of God is moving, the results can be both messy and thrilling at the same time.

Convergence starts in our home, moves to the neighborhood and eventually to the whole city. While Christ is being lifted up and churches are adding to their membership rolls, the truth is that there is little citywide focus in the Body of Christ. This is primarily because modern churches see themselves as independent of one another. This is partly the result of not realizing that we are baptized into one body and the Ekklesia is

His Body. It is also the simple result of people building their own programs or platforms individually, rather than fellowshipping with all believers in a region. We are all brothers and sisters in Christ and one family in Him.

Much of the normal "church" activity in a western city is reshuffling the deck or competing. This is generally the result of consumer programs that encourage people to fill seats and "buy" ministry services from the professional ministers.

What does it take to reach a city?

Causing a city-centric movement requires a growing percentage of the people in the city becoming connected with Christ-centered communities and having faith-building encounters with Jesus Christ. He will energize us with His purpose when we receive Him and offer Him our lives.

Movement can be measured by the percentage of new believers in a city growing faster than the population. This ultimately impacts the whole quality of life in the city. The real measurement, however, is life transformations as people are rapidly conformed to the image of Christ. New believers are immediately encouraged to begin sharing the testimony of their encounter with Christ and are trained to make disciples who make disciples.

A citywide convergence to the individual Lordship and corporate Headship of Christ is an organic thing. It's the Spiritual energy of God's glory unleashed across a city and overtaking man-made denominational borders. There's no one church, no one organization, no one leader in charge. People that try to take ownership will simply be bypassed by the river of God's glory as He moves around them to accomplish His purpose in bringing liberty to the captives.

Paul told the Corinthian believers that when we are separated by denominationalism we are acting like mere mortals. The object is to come under the universal Headship of Jesus Christ. That is the Convergence of God's will among us. There are different streams that all converge to become a river of God's will and purpose.

As we each respond to the will of God in our lives, we are aligned with His ancient relational pathway. The Holy Spirit is revealing the Father's heart to us for one another and to our neighbors. As we respond to His leading, He will direct us each into new spheres of influence and networks of relationships through "persons of peace."

We are bringing the message of freedom to the captives of the wicked one. Once our homes, neighborhoods, and cities come into the revelation of Jesus Christ, the Holy Spirit will be reaching the nations. It is a process that works from one person to the next, until we are all one Body under the Headship of our Lord and Savior, Jesus Christ.

> "Therefore, since we have this ministry, as we have received mercy, we do not lose heart. But we have renounced the hidden things of shame, not walking in craftiness nor handling the word of God deceitfully, but by manifestation of the truth commending ourselves to every man's conscience in the sight of God. But even if our gospel is veiled, it is veiled to those who are perishing, whose minds the god of this age has blinded, who do not believe, lest the light of the gospel of the glory of Christ, who is the image of God, should shine on them.
>
> For we do not preach ourselves, but Christ Jesus the Lord, and ourselves your bondservants for Jesus' sake. For it is the God who commanded light to shine out of darkness, who has shone in our hearts to give the light of the knowledge of the glory of God in the face of Jesus Christ." **2 Corinthians 4:1-6**

Footnote Sources and Scripture References

All Strong's Concordance references refer to their respective lexicon identifiers.

1. Ephesians 3:10

2. John 8:36

3. Strong's #2776

4. http://exegetist-theberean.blogspot.com/2007/05/kepale-meanings.html

5. 2 Corinthians 4:17

6. Strong's #1537

7. Matthew 16:17-18

8. Strong's #3619

9. Daniel 12:4

10. Psalm 37:23

11. John 3:8

12. 2 Samuel 11

13. http://pioneernt.wordpress.com/2012/04/25/word-study-142-you-you-all-and-each-of-you/

14. Strong's #4982

15. Strong's #4004

16. James Rutz, Mega Shift, Igniting Spiritual Power (Colorado Springs, Co: Empowerment Press, 2005), 25-27.

17. Strong's #3642

18. Strong's #1504

Footnotes

19. http://www.patheos.com/blogs/jesuscreed/2005/04/13/tols toy-and-eikons-of-god/

20. Strong's #H430

21. Genesis 25:29

22. Genesis 3:6

23. Strong's #2222

24. Ephesians 4:16

25. Strong's #4563

26. 2 Corinthians 4:7

27. 2 Samuel 16:12

28. Ezekiel 36:36

29. Strong's #3653

30. Romans 12:1

31. Strong's #3339

32. Philippians 3:20

33. http://en.wikipedia.org/wiki/Wave_packet

34. Strong's #3340

35. Strong's #1922

36. 2 Corinthians 9:6 & Romans 5:17

37. Myles, Dr. Francis (2011-03-27). The Order of Melchizedek: Rediscovering the Eternal Priesthood of Jesus Christ and How It Affects Us Today (Kindle Locations 875-876). Word and Spirit Resources. Kindle Edition.

38. 2 Peter 3:10

39. Genesis 1:26

40. Strong's #2842

Footnotes

41. Colossians 2:9

42. Colossians 2:9-19

43. Luke 4:1-13

44. Colossians 1:27

45. Galatians 2:20

46. Luke 10:27 & Matthew 28:16

47. 1 Corinthians 2:9-16

48. Strong's #5043

49. Strong's #5206

50. Don Walker, "Understanding „Sonship" by Don Walker, "Lifehouse International Ministries" http://www.lifehouseinc.net/tp42/page.asp?id=197503

51. Scott, James M., ed. "Adoption as Sons of God—an Exegetical Investigation into the Background of UIOQESIA in the Pauline Corpus." Wissenschaftliche Untersuchungen zum Neuen Testament 2.48 (1992): xv+353.

52. Romans 8:22

53. http://www.whatifenterprises.com/whatif/whatiskairos.pdf

54. Strong's #4482

55. 2 Corinthians 2:14

56. 1 John 1:7

57. Genesis 1:26

58. 1 Corinthians 2:16

59. Strong's #3661

60. 1 Corinthians 15

61. 2 Corinthians 5:8

Footnotes

62. Ephesians 3:10

63. Romans 1:16

64. Strong's #3129

65. Oldenburg, Ray. 1989. The Great Good Place. New York: Paragon House: 3-42.

66. http://www.cs.unm.edu/~sheppard/proxemics.htm

67. Jacob Neusner, From Politics to Piety: The Emergence of Pharisaic Judaism (Englewood Cliffs, NJ: Prentice Hall, 1973), see also his "Two Picture of the Pharisees: Philosophical Circle or Eating Club," Anglican Theological Review 64 (1982): 525-57.

68. Strong's #2784

69. Strong's #2097

70. Strong's #1256

71. Ephesians 4:11-13

72. D.W. Fowlkes, 'Developing a Church Planting Movement in India' (PhD thesis, University of Free State, 2004), p. 53

73. Acts 19:6

74. Galatians 4:6

75. http://en.wikipedia.org/wiki/Pareto_principle

* There is a wealth of information from T Austin Sparks from the 1920-1950's in which he introduced the eternal purpose paradigm as a lens to view the Scriptures.

** The paradigm of body life and the plural dynamic of the Godhead has been very well discussed by Milt Rodriguez of The Rebuilders:. http://miltrodriguez.wordpress.com.

** Read more on individualism: Common Ground: An Introduction to Eastern Christianity for the American Christian. Chapter 11. Light and Life Publishing Company, Minneapolis, Minnesota. 1991

Christ Centered Community Discipleship Training "GO" WORKSHOPS

CON**V**ERGENCE
@ JESUS LABS

The "GO" workshop-based training that is both interactive and instructive. The object is to conduct these workshops in third place environments. It is easier to see ourselves duplicating a process when it is taught in our own contexts and environments.

Phase 1 - Training – Vision

- **Making First Follower Leaders**
- **Intentional 4th Generation Disciple Making**
- **Equipping and Releasing Disciple Makers**
- **Spirit-led Lifestyle Ministry**
- **Developing A Kingdom Culture**

Phase 2 – Equipping & Training

- **Multiplying Movement Strategies**
- **Spirit Led Communities That Multiply**
- **Scripture Based Supernatural Worldview**
- **Rest Based Spiritual Warfare In The Heavenlies**
- **Living in the Spirit of Life**
- **Recognizing, Equipping and Releasing Spiritual Gifts and Functions**

Equipping For Apostolic Lifestyles

Jesus Labs is an alliance of believers moving in the all things ministry of Christ. Ministry is conducted in the daily rhythms of our respective lives as we live out an apostolic schedule.

The Lord orchestrates divine appointments that order our days and supernatural assignments are the norm. Every day is an adventure of learning, revelation and increase.

We are moving and adapting to bring Jesus into context with unbelievers so they can experience His reality in their lives.

It is our hearts desire to grow in intimacy with God and to bring all men into a life-changing encounter with the Lord Jesus Christ. Unbelievers are still drawn to Jesus Christ today as they were before the cross. He is as much present with us today as in the first century.

Tell us God's vision for your life and we will prayerfully assist you to be positioned for the fullness of God's will and purpose and to have every resource necessary to accomplish God's plan for your life.

WWW.JESUSLABS.ORG

**3651 East Baseline Rd Suite E203
Gilbert, AZ 85234**

CONVERGENCE
@ JESUS LABS

www.ingramcontent.com/pod-product-compliance
Lightning Source LLC
LaVergne TN
LVHW051517080426
835509LV00017B/2091